Remembering
Martin Luther King, Jr.

His Life and Crusade in Pictures

Charles Johnson and Bob Adelman

This book is dedicated to Martin Luther King, Jr.,
to his dream of a beloved community, and to the selfless
activists who brought that dream closer for all of us.

3 3083 00567 3733

LIFE Books
Editor **Robert Sullivan**
President **Andrew Blau**

Bob Adelman Books Inc.
Introduction and Essays **Charles Johnson**
Editor **Christopher Sweet**
Photography and Caption Editor **Bob Adelman**
Art Director **Rick DeMonico**
Digital Imaging **Stephen Watt**
Research **Jill Chang**

Time Inc. Home Entertainment
Publisher **Richard Fraiman**
General Manager **Steven Sandonato**
Executive Director, Marketing Services **Carol Pittard**
Director, Retail & Special Sales **Tom Mifsud**
Director, New Product Development **Peter Harper**
Assistant Director, Brand Marketing **Laura Adam**
Associate Counsel **Helen Wan**
Book Production Manager **Suzanne Janso**
Design & Prepress Manager **Anne-Michelle Gallero**
Senior Brand Manager Marketing Manager **Joy Butts**
Senior Brand Manager, TWRS/M **Holly Oakes**
Associate Brand Manager **Shelley Rescober**

Special Thanks to:
Glenn Buonocore
Susan Chodakiewicz
Margaret Hess
Robert Marasco
Dennis Marcel
Brooke Reger
Mary Sarro-Waite
Ilene Schreider
Adriana Tierno
Alex Voznesenskiy

Published by Time Inc. Home Entertainment Books
LIFE is a trademark of Time Inc.

Time Inc.
1271 Avenue of the Americas
New York, New York 10020

We welcome your comments and suggestions about TIHE Books.
Please write to us at:
TIHE Books
Attention: Book Editors
PO Box 11016
Des Moines, IA 50336-1016

If you would like to order any of our hardcover Collector's
Edition books, please call us at 1-800-327-6388.
(Monday through Friday, 7:00 a.m.— 8:00 p.m. or Saturday,
7:00 a.m.— 6:00 p.m. Central Time).

INTRODUCTION

The life and legacy of Martin Luther King, Jr., permeates—in ways great and small, direct and indirect—every facet of our social and political world. Although he was assassinated forty years ago, his hypnotic voice and unique vision linger, ghostlike, in the background of every conversation that touches upon race, the state of black America, and this nation's multiracial future. His name, an eponym given to streets and community centers, is invoked these days with the piety (and emotional distance) reserved for this republic's Founders, and well it should be, for King was a revolutionary whose deeds created the structure, the texture, and the tone of the society in which we live.

Yet in some ways his posthumous visibility renders his life—and the high drama of the noble, world-altering movement he symbolized—largely invisible to the generations born after 1968. This, of course, is the price of canonization. Vaguely, we remember a little something of his many southern campaigns (but seldom all the principal players) and his ever-broadening agenda for global peace and economic justice, but with each passing decade the details grow a bit fainter. Indeed, some are forgotten entirely, lost as King is airbrushed, reinterpreted, packaged, and repackaged by those on the left and right (even those terms have a different meaning than they did during King's era), by liberals and conservatives, by everyone from Afro-centrists to those who use his memory to oppose programs, such as affirmative action, that he would approve. How soon we forget that King was not only a civil rights activist, but also this country's preeminent moral philosopher, a spiritual aspirant, a father and a husband, and that these diverse roles—these multiple dimensions of his too brief life—were the foundations for his singular "dream" that inspired millions worldwide.

It is our hope that this beautiful collection of images taken by some of America's leading photographers will serve readers eager to time travel, to project themselves back into the most transformative decades this country has experienced after the Civil War and to better appreciate the complexity, genius, and memorable public ministry of Martin Luther King, Jr., as he journeyed from Montgomery to Memphis. Each and every photo on the pages that follow is a portal—a doorway—into a watershed life produced by America's ongoing, unfinished experiment in democracy.

Enter, enjoy, and be enlightened.

Charles Johnson, Seattle

EARLY YEARS

It is quite easy for me to think of the universe as basically friendly mainly because of my uplifting hereditary and environmental circumstances.

Martin Luther King, Jr.,
An Autobiography of Religious Development, 1950.

Leafing through the King family album, we see, on the right, an early photograph. Standing are, from left to right, King's mother, father, and maternal grandmother. Seated are Alfred Daniel (A. D.), Christine, and Martin.

Twenty-one-year-old Martin Luther King, Jr., often spoke glowingly of his childhood and youth as years of fulfillment when "I had no basic problems or burdens." His was "a family where love was central and where lovely relationships were ever present," and he would have no doubt identified his predecessors and peers with the dedication in the late writer Ralph Ellison's second novel, *Juneteenth*: "To That Vanished Tribe into Which I Was Born: The American Negroes."

They were a different breed.

When King was born on January 15, 1929, only nine months before the stock market crash, at 501 Auburn Avenue N.E. in a two-story Queen Anne-style home in Atlanta, he entered a family only sixty-four years removed from the devastating experience of slavery—a family that could boast of producing three generations of black preachers before his birth. His grandfather, Adam Daniel (A. D.) Williams (the son of a Greene County slave-preacher), transformed a struggling little church, Ebenezer Baptist, into a prominent institution with nine hundred members, wed in 1899 Jennie Celeste Parks, a gentle woman who briefly attended Spelman Seminary, and led numerous organizations dedicated to political and racial progress. No less an activist was King père, a man who knew and inveighed against injustice and racism his entire life.

In the home of these pious black men and women, who deeply valued education and whom he saw indefatigably engaged in social work and spiritual practice (the social gospel), young Martin—a child of the black church—found it "quite easy for me to lean more toward optimism than pessimism about human nature." By his own admission, he was "precocious," a questioning boy who at age thirteen "shocked my Sunday School class by denying the bodily resurrection of Jesus." He felt uneasy with the uncritical fundamentalism of the Baptist faith, only joined the church at age five because his older sister did so and he did not want her to get ahead of him in anything, and he never experienced the "crisis moment" associated with religious conversion.

Of course, he saw poverty and hardscrabble lives during the Great Depression. And he knew prejudice as a child. His first exposure to a "race problem" occurred when the father of one of his white playmates broke up their friendship, an event that made six-year-old Martin "determined to hate every white person" until he went away to college and met Caucasians of good will—as well as liberal professors like Benjamin E. Mays, president of Morehouse College, who provided him with the intellectual example of a modern minister he hoped to adopt as his own model.

In 1944, when King was fifteen, he won a contest for a speech entitled "The Negro and the Constitution." Even then, the ensorceling orator he would become can be glimpsed in the acuity of his conclusion, where he said, "My heart throbs anew in the hope that…[America] will cast down the last barrier to perfect freedom. And I with my brother of blackest hue, possessing at last my rightful heritage and holding my head erect, may stand beside the Saxon—a Negro—and yet a man!"

Yet Martin's academic record at Morehouse was, as his teacher George D. Kelsey put it, "short of what may be called 'good.'" Mays was even less enthusiastic, stating in a letter of reference for Martin and another pupil that "they are not brilliant students but they have good minds." King's gradepoint average was 2.48, between C+ and B. That less-than-stellar performance was most likely due to the social distractions he found and a desire to cut loose a little when he started college—he was, after all, only fifteen when he began. But by his senior year Martin, who had considered pursuing careers in either law or medicine, sparked to his studies; he was ordained as an associate pastor at Ebenezer at age nineteen, his calling being

"…not a miraculous or supernatural something; on the contrary it was an inner urge calling me to serve humanity. I guess the influence of my father also had a great deal to do with my going into the ministry."

Martin struggled to find his path at Morehouse, but by the time he reached Crozer Theological Seminary in Chester, Pennsylvania, he buckled down. He wrote to his beloved grandmother that "I never go anywhere much but in these books." His diligence paid off. He became the president of the student body, delivered the valedictory address at his commencement ceremony, received a J. Lewis Crozer Fellowship of $1,200, and the Pearl Plafker Memorial Award as the student who "in the judgment of the faculty, has been the outstanding member of his class during his course in the seminary."

At Boston University's Graduate School, he studied with Edgar Brightman and L. Harold DeWolf, pursuing the philosophy he later would say he found more persuasive than any other, Personalism, which emphasized personality as the supreme value and the key to the meaning of reality. By the time Martin earned his Ph.D. on June 5, 1955, his pansophical education was complete (according to Julian Bond, King could recite whole passages of Plato from memory); he had married a beautiful New England Conservatory student named Coretta Scott; and he had accepted the pastorate at Dexter Avenue Baptist Church in Montgomery, Alabama (with the highest salary, $4,800 yearly, of any minister in the city). Beyond all doubt, this remarkable, disciplined, profoundly spiritual young man knew at the age of twenty-five that "Religion for me is life."

MONTGOMERY

A charismatic young leader emerges

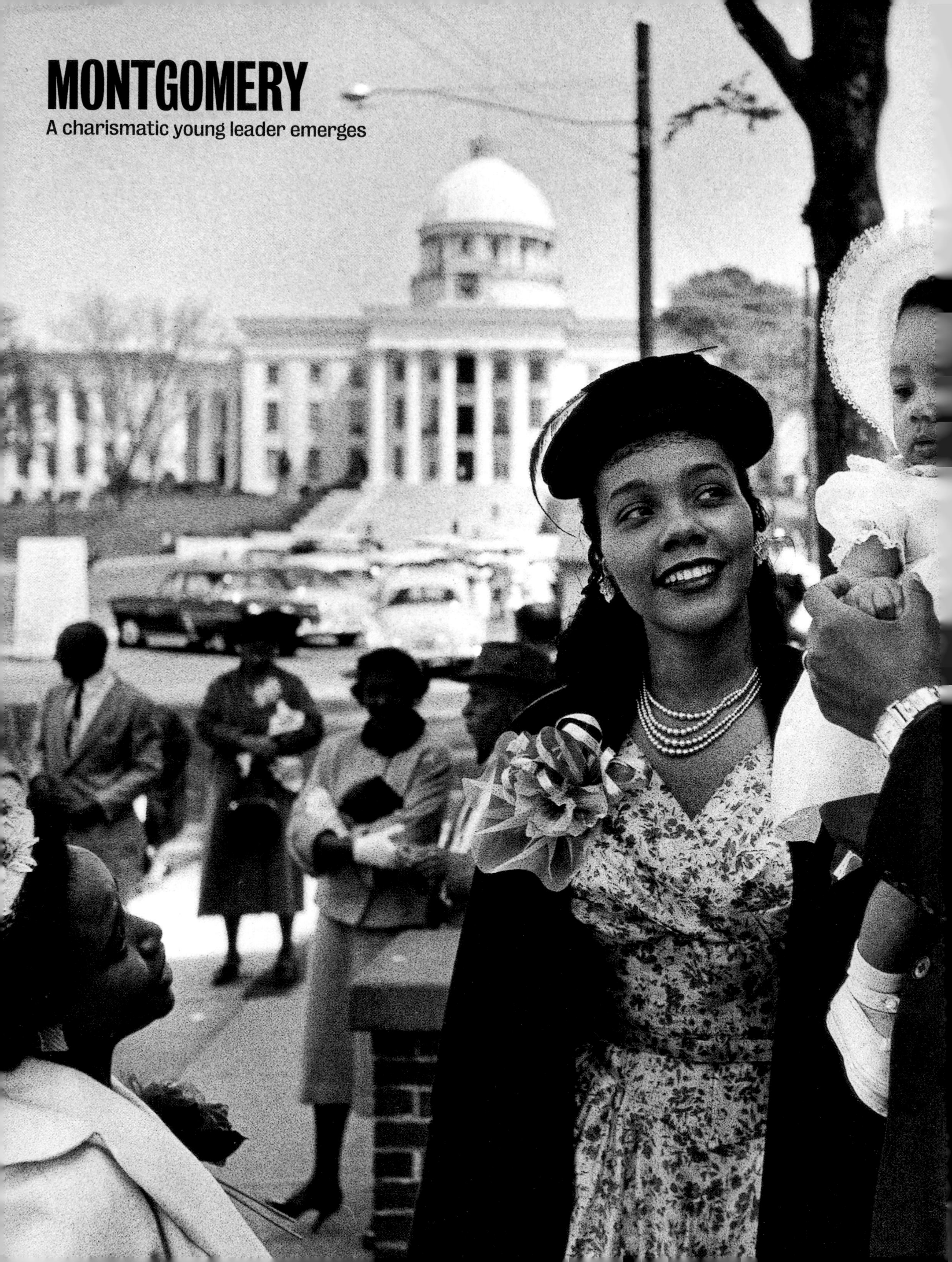

Proud pastor and new father, Dr. King, accompanied by his wife, Coretta, shows off his baby daughter, Yolanda.

Above, right: Dr. King greets members of his congregation on the steps outside Dexter Avenue Baptist Church.

Right: Rosa Parks, whose refusal to give up her seat on a city bus to a white rider triggered the bus boycott, is fingerprinted on February 22, 1956, after her second arrest, for boycotting.

Mass meetings kept boycotters abreast of developments, unified them, and strengthened their resolve. At first meetings were held twice weekly, then more frequently as the boycott continued. Here King leads a gathering at the First Baptist Church.

MONTGOMERY
A charismatic young leader emerges

Christ gave us the goals and Mahatma Gandhi the tactics.

Martin Luther King, Jr.,
Montgomery, 1955

The watershed event for which King's entire life had been a hurtling preparation arrived on December 1, 1955, when a 42-year-old seamstress and secretary of the Montgomery branch of the National Association for the Advancement of Colored People (NAACP) named Rosa Parks refused to give up her seat to a white man in the black section of a crowded bus. One year earlier the U. S. Supreme Court had ruled in *Brown v. Board of Education of To-peka* that racial segregation in public schools was unconstitutional, but it took Parks's arrest to electrify and unify the fifty thousand black men and women of Montgomery around an epic 382-day bus boycott.

King met often with other Montgomery Improvement Association (MIA) leaders to avert violence, solve transportation problems, and work out strategies to counter the city's efforts to stop the boycott.

King, who had been in the "Cradle of the Confederacy" for only twenty months, was elected president of the Montgomery Improvement Association (MIA), which spearheaded the boycott, although later he replaced that term with a more Thoreauvian and philosophically expansive phrase, "massive noncooperation with evil." On the boycott's first day, King thundered to five thousand people at the Holt Street Baptist Church, "If you will protest courageously, and yet with dignity and Christian love, future historians will say, 'There lived a great people—a black people—who injected new meaning and dignity into the veins of civilization.'"

Inspired by their ministers, who held two mass meetings weekly, and by the unleashed genie of their own power to turn city buses into empty, ghostlike shells rumbling down roads at an eventual loss of $250,000 to the city, black people walked wherever they had to go. Some rode mules. Or turned to horse-drawn buggies. Students at Alabama State College hitched rides. Three hundred cars were donated and ten black churches helped purchase station wagons to create a car pool, each with the name of a church emblazoned on its sides.

Their example inspired people worldwide. Donations to bolster the boycott poured in from across America, as well as from Tokyo and Switzerland, but Montgomery's whites, who at first expected the boycott to fail, refused to honor the MIA's demands, which had been drawn up by Rev. Ralph Abernathy. In a show of racial solidarity, the mayor and his commissioners joined the White Citizens' Council. City officials declared mass rides in black cabs illegal. In retaliation,

King's eloquence and peaceful, dignified bearing served as a model for the protesters and lifted their spirits. Here he greets a supporter. One elderly woman who walked every day told King, "My feet is tired but my soul is rested."

King was arrested twice, for speeding and for his participation in the boycott. On some days the telephone at his home rang thirty or forty times, with callers spewing obscenities at him and his family.

One such vicious call proved to be of pivotal importance for King. His phone rang in the middle of the night. The caller said this: "Listen, nigger, we've taken all we want from you. Before next week you'll be sorry you ever came to Montgomery. If you aren't out of this town in three days we're gonna blow your brains out and blow up your house." Right then he almost despaired. King walked to the kitchen and made himself a cup of coffee. He sat down at the table and prayed, "Lord....I am at the end of my powers. I have nothing left. I can't face it alone." Then, in the stillness of the night, in the mounting "crisis moment" that was Montgomery, he felt the divine, transforming presence that had eluded him since childhood. When King stood up he was renewed, certain of the righteousness—and successful outcome—of the cause.

His famous "kitchen conversion" came none too soon. On January 30, 1956, while King was at a meeting, his home was bombed. He rushed there, found Coretta and their baby, Yolanda, unharmed, and outside an angry, armed black crowd spoiling for a showdown with white policemen at the scene. The situation was edging toward violence. He raised one hand to quiet the crowd. He said, "I want you to go home and put down your weapons. We cannot solve this problem through retaliatory violence. We must meet violence with nonviolence…We must meet hate with love."

Later the policemen would say King saved their lives, for the crowd heard his counsel—indeed, King's Gandhi-esque stance, his agapic vision, were heard round the world as something uniquely redemptive in the bloody, centuries-long struggle for black liberation in America. However, after a year of sacrifices, after a war of nerves that included blacks being beaten and dragged from MIA vehicles and the bombing of black gas stations, the protesters began to tire.

Above: *On the evening of January 30, 1956, King's house was bombed. Fortunately his wife and baby daughter were uninjured. Told of the bombing, Dr. King rushed home from a mass meeting to be with his family. Here, flanked by city officials, he calms a crowd that gathered outside his home.*

Opposite: *In February 1956, the police take a mug shot of a stony-faced Dr. King, arrested for the second time in his life for his boycott activities (the first was less than a month earlier on a minor traffic violation as part of the city's "get tough" policy). Under an obscure state anti-labor law, a grand jury indicted ninety boycott leaders, including ministers and car-pool drivers. The arrests were a futile effort on the part of the city to end the boycott and only helped unify the black community.*

King and ninety leaders were indicted by a Montgomery grand jury, which resurrected a hoary state law that prohibited boycotts. The MIA responded by expanding its demands to a call for complete integration, and it was aided by Bayard Rustin and Stanley Levison—the beginning of two long and fruitful friendships for King. In August of that year, he testified with three hundred others before the Platform and Resolutions Committee at the Democratic National Convention in Chicago that "The question of civil rights is one of the supreme moral issues of our time."

The protesters suffered a major setback on October 30, 1956, when the city's legal department stopped carpooling by blacks. Many feared that move might unravel the resistance; in fact, it did demoralize many. But on November 13, the U. S. Supreme Court ruled that segregation on buses was unconstitutional. To be sure, that victory by Montgomery's black citizens triggered more violence—blacks were attacked, buses were shot at, and Abernathy's home and church were bombed—yet when the city's white leaders denounced these criminal acts they ended. On December 20, King declared that the boycott was over and once again provided the language needed to heal wounds on both sides: "We must seek an integration based on mutual respect. As we go back to the buses, let us be loving enough to turn an enemy into a friend."

Opposite: *"Sole power" brought many blacks to and from work and around the city. Here a woman carries a box of turnip greens on her head.*

Left: *At a popular pickup spot, boycotters wait for rides in car pools, cabs, and station wagons, making use of the improvised transit system that the MIA organized to replace city buses.*

Below: *City buses were soon idle and service was stopped a few months after the boycott began. The financial burden that resulted from losing so many of the riders crippled the bus company.*

The Kings cross the street during a lunch break at the conspiracy-to-boycott trial. King was arrested with other leaders under an archaic law as part of the city's effort to end the boycott.

On March 22, 1956, King celebrates his conviction. He believed it was right to disobey unjust laws. Explaining his buoyant mood, he said, "Ordinarily, a person leaving a courtroom with a conviction behind him would wear a somber face. But I left with a smile. I knew that I was a convicted criminal, but I was proud of my crime."

Above: *More than a year after the boycott began, the U. S. Supreme Court ruled that Alabama's bus segregation laws were unconstitutional. Martin Luther King, Jr., waits to board the city's first integrated bus.*

Opposite: *Sitting in the front of the bus, Dr. King enjoys the fruits of the victory—color-blind service on the city's buses. The time had come, as King had said at the mass meeting the previous night, "to move from protest to reconciliation."*

On September 3, 1958, almost two years after triumphantly leading the battle to end bus segregation in Montgomery, King is wrongfully arrested outside the city's courthouse for loitering as he waits to attend a trial and is then man-handled down to the police station. He raises a hand to warn off supporters from intervening.

While a concerned Coretta looks on, her husband is booked. King later said the policemen had "tried to break my arm; they grabbed my collar and tried to choke me, and when they got me to the cell, they kicked me in." Once King's identity became known to the police, he was released on his own recognizance. Later he was tried and convicted, and he resolved to go to jail. The police commissioner paid his fine ($14) to keep the incident out of the news, and a frustrated King was once again released.

PRAYER PILGRIMAGE

King steps onto the national stage

Roy Wilkins, Martin Luther King, Jr., and A. Philip Randolph pose in front of the Statue of Lincoln inside the Memorial.

As the crowd cheers him on, Martin Luther King, Jr., in clerical robes, strides to the rostrum.

King's rousing plea, "Give us the ballot, give us the ballot," moved the crowd and caught the attention of the press in his first national address.

PRAYER PILGRIMAGE
King steps onto the national stage

A man who hits his peak at twenty-seven has a tough job ahead.

Martin Luther King, Jr.,
New York Post interview,
April 14, 1957

In a magnificent photograph, young King—the lionized symbol of black America's victory in Montgomery—stands in the Lincoln Memorial between two towering representatives of the fight against racial discrimination. At left is Roy Wilkins of the NAACP, the other is A. Philip Randolph, organizer of the Brotherhood of Sleeping Car Porters union. They are at the Prayer Pilgrimage for Freedom in Washington, D.C., on May 17, 1957, and the moment is clearly a triumphant and yet tenuous coalescing of efforts by America's two major civil rights organizations.

For in that photo, King represents a spanking-new group, the direct-action-oriented Southern Christian Leadership Conference (SCLC), created at a meeting on February 14 and dedicated to opposing all forms of segregation and to fighting for black voter registration in the South. It was church-based and defined by its philosophy of nonviolence and non-cooperation with unjust laws. It was also perceived by some officials of the NAACP to be a potential threat to the older organization's financial base in the South (in churches especially), to its membership, and to its legal approach. At the time of its formation, a Pittsburgh Courier editorial queried, "Are the organizers of the Southern Christian Leadership Conference implying by their action that the NAACP is no longer capable of doing what it has been doing for decades....What sound reason is there for having two organizations with the same goal when one has been doing such an effective job?"

From the very first days of the SCLC, its leadership took great pains to overcome the NAACP's opposition. (Rev. Joseph Lowery recalled a meeting in New York with him, King, Abernathy, Wilkins, John Morsell, and Gloster Current, during which Current remarked, "To tell you the truth, gentlemen, at the end of the bus boycott, you all should have disbanded everything, and been back in the NAACP.") Yet, although the two organizations differed in methods (some argued that the Montgomery boycott's success was ultimately the result not of mass movement confrontation but of the kind of legal and lawful tactics that the NAACP had always championed), they shared identical goals and the SCLC's founders were all NAACP members.

Thus it was incumbent upon the younger group to convince the older one that their approaches were complementary, not competitive. Where one worked through the courts, they argued, the other engaged in community action that enforced those legal victories. King and other MIA members took out lifetime NAACP memberships, and King urged members of the Dexter Avenue Baptist Church to do the same. Well into the 1960s King spoke at NAACP fund-raisers. Whenever possible the two groups tried to raise funds together, then split the proceeds, and some SCLC literature stated (for the NAACP's sake) that it was not trying to set up local units or draw individual memberships. Indeed, in his speech at the Prayer Pilgrimage, King emphasized to the crowd of thirty-seven thousand gathered before the Lincoln Memorial that "We have won marvelous victories through the work of the NAACP....[It] has done more to achieve civil rights for Negroes than any other organization we can point to."

Yet, despite these conciliatory moves aimed at cooperation, in another photo in which a smiling King walks to the podium to speak, with people cheering him and raising their hands in salute, we notice a rather sad-faced Roy Wilkins still sitting and staring at the camera—a portent perhaps of brewing problems that would intensify over the next decade between these two outstanding civil rights leaders.

Above: *As the organized events of the day draw to a close, hundreds surround the charismatic King, hoping for an autograph, a handshake, or a chance to have their photograph taken beside him. To King's right, Martin Luther King, Sr., holding a camera, proudly trails his son.*

Nevertheless, the Prayer Pilgrimage was a shining hour for King. It was his first speech before a national audience, an address aimed at demonstrating black solidarity, raising a nation's conscience on racial justice, and appealing to the Eisenhower administration to pass the Civil Rights Bill stalled in committees by southern politicians. (And surely it was influential in nudging Congress to establish that September the Civil Rights Commission and a new Civil Rights Division in the Department of Justice.) King was introduced by 68-year-old A. Philip Randolph, one of his idols and a leader in the labor movement, editor of the outspoken Messenger, and, as a fighter for equality for thirty years, one of the elder statesmen of the black liberation struggle.

"Give us the ballot," King said in remarks that revealed the struggles of the civil rights movement to be a continuation of the Civil War and black suffrage the fulfillment of Lincoln's vision. "We come humbly to say to the men in the forefront of our government that the civil rights issue is…an eternal moral issue which may well determine the destiny of our nation in the ideological struggle with communism….We must act now, before it is too late."

Following spread: So enthusiastic became the crowd—people always seemed to want to reach out and shake King's hand—that when the Pilgrimage ended police had to step in and escort him to safety.

HARLEM
STABBING
Living under
constant threat

I'm so happy that you didn't sneeze.

Letter from a ninth-grade
white student, 1958

King's post-Montgomery period was, of course, not without danger. On September 20, 1958, he was autographing copies of his first book, *Stride Toward Freedom*, in Blumstein's Department Store on 125th Street in Harlem when a black woman, Izola Ware Curry, stabbed him almost fatally near his heart with a Japanese letter opener. He was taken to Harlem Hospital, where Dr. Aubre D. Maynard removed two of his ribs to get the knife out. "If you had sneezed during all the hours of waiting," Maynard said, "your aorta would have been punctured and you would have drowned in your own blood." He cut a small incision over King's heart. Permanent scar tissue formed in the shape of a cross. "He is a minister," the doctor explained. "It seemed appropriate."

King refused to press charges against the woman who attacked him. He told the authorities, "Don't do anything to her; don't prosecute her; get her healed." Curry was committed to an institution for the criminally insane.

As he convalesced, King received thousands of sympathy letters and cards from around the world. "What makes you think you are the 'exclusive property' of the Negro race only?" a white woman wrote. "You belong to us too, because we love you. Please don't lose faith in us 'whites.' There are many of us who are good and pray for your triumph."

While King was promoting his new book, a woman walked up to him and asked, "Are you Dr. King?" "Yes, I am," he said. She then drove a seven-inch letter opener into his chest. Opposite: A bystander daubs blood from King's hand, which was also injured in the attack, as he waits for an ambulance to arrive.

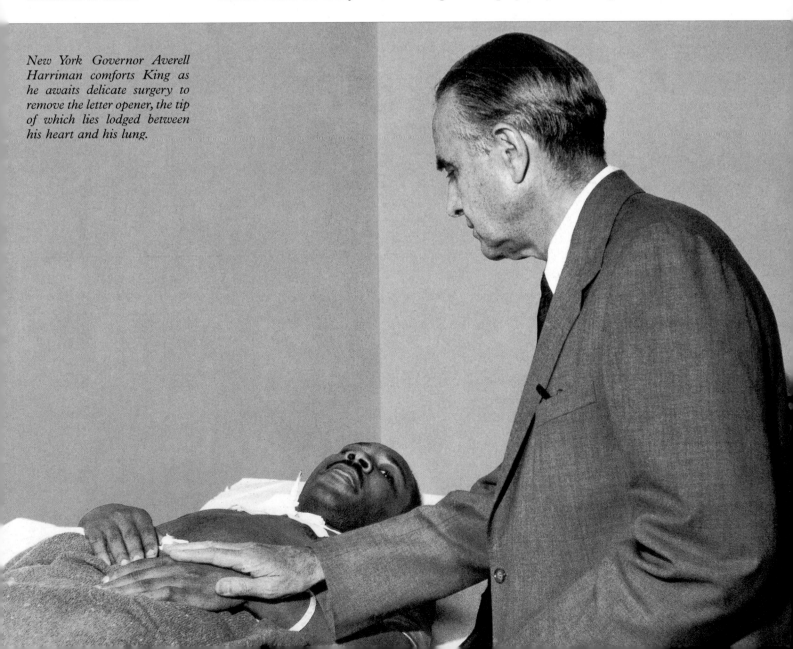

New York Governor Averell Harriman comforts King as he awaits delicate surgery to remove the letter opener, the tip of which lies lodged between his heart and his lung.

Following a three-hour operation to remove the letter opener, during which two of King's ribs were removed, Dr. Emil A. Naclerio examines the patient. Two days after the successful operation, King was back in danger. He developed pneumonia. By the next morning he was on the mend.

Ten days after the attack, a convalescing King cheerfully poses with his mother and his wife at a Harlem Hospital news conference.

Coretta Scott King kisses her husband as he is released from Harlem Hospital.

On October 24, 1958, more than a month after he was stabbed, King waves to a large group of friends and neighbors assembled on the tarmac at Montgomery Airport. His full recovery took two more months.

LIFE IN ATLANTA
Husband, father, crusader, author, and pastor

We must do a good job, irrespective of race, and do it so well that nobody can do it better.

Martin Luther King, Jr.

It was with great reluctance that King resigned as pastor at Dexter Avenue Baptist Church and returned to Atlanta. He loved those in Montgomery who had fought side by side with him to break the yoke of segregation. But in the wake of that internationally celebrated victory, King was tired and felt the toll of sacrifices for the movement on his personal life. "As a result of my leadership in the Montgomery movement," he told the parishioners at Dexter, "my duties and activities tripled. A multiplicity of new responsibilities poured in upon me in almost staggering torrents. So I ended up futilely attempting to be four or five men in one."

His family returned to Atlanta on February 1, 1960. The scant few years after the Montgomery boycott had seen the birth of his son Martin Luther King III and his trip in 1957 to Africa for ceremonies celebrating Ghana's independence (King recognized early that the fights against colonialism and American segregation were the same, but also called the "Afro-American…a true hybrid, a combination of two cultures") and to India in 1959. *Jet* magazine estimated that in 1958 alone King delivered 208 speeches and traveled 780,000 miles.

Even at rest, between movement campaigns, King remained extraordinarily busy. The world showered him with job offers, speaking requests, and awards, among them the NAACP's Spingarn Medal, presented at his alma mater Morehouse College. At this event, his former teacher Benjamin Mays said of King, "Because you did not seek fame, it has come to you. It must have been a person like you that Emerson had in mind when he said, 'See how the masses of men worry themselves into nameless graves when here and there a great, unselfish soul forgets himself into immortality.' You are gentle and loving, Christian and brave, sane and wise."

Those words, perhaps more than any others, reveal the pre- and post-Montgomery character of King. As Jesse Jackson said in the 1990s, "He was a family man," although his one great regret in life was that he seldom had much time to devote to his beloved wife and children. He was raised to be a Race Man, but also to be something young militants in the 1960s derided as corny—"a credit to his Race," which in King's case translated beautifully into an ongoing personal struggle for perfection and personal responsibility. At Crozer Seminary, he knew his each and every deed would be seen by whites as either a "credit" or a "demerit" for his people. Recollecting those days, King said, "If I were a minute late to class, I was almost morbidly conscious of it and sure that everyone noticed it. Rather than be thought of as always laughing, I'm afraid I was grimly serious for a time. I had a tendency to overdress, to keep my room spotless, my shoes perfectly shined, and my clothes immaculately pressed."

He preferred casual dress to those conservative dark suits he wore in public—for the public, one might say. He took to heart his own advice that "We shall have to create leaders who embody virtues we can respect." According to his wife, he genuinely was uninterested in money and material success and wished he could take a vow of poverty. "Martin always tried to eliminate from our lives all things we could do without," she said. He always felt that in order to serve his people fully he needed time for study. After his trip to India, King returned home committed to devoting one day a week to silence and meditation—that was one of his

King removes a charred cross from his front lawn as his son Marty watches. The previous night, April 25, 1960, crosses had been burned at many black homes in Atlanta. Ku Klux Klan Night Riders burned crosses to intimidate, frighten, and warn blacks intent on asserting their rights.

King was once asked by his daughter Yolanda, pictured with him at left, why she could not go to Funtown, a popular amusement park in Atlanta. Of the occasion, he remembered, "One of the most painful experiences I have ever faced was to see her tears when I told her Funtown was closed to colored children, for I realized the first dark cloud of inferiority had floated into her little mental sky."

reasons for moving back to Atlanta, and he conditioned himself to get by on just four hours of sleep a night. But always his off-the-clock schedule took priority over King's hope for deepening his spiritual and intellectual practices.

At home, away from the camera, he worked on sermons that took two-thirds of a day to compose. One of his favorites was "The Three Dimensions of a Complete Life," which he delivered in London just before receiving the Nobel Peace Prize. He also composed speeches that looked critically inward at the black community and its promise as well as outward toward the shortcomings of the white world. "We must work on two fronts," he said. "On the one hand we must continually resist the system of segregation—the system which is the basic cause of our lagging standards; on the other hand, we must work constructively to improve

Coretta is upset that her husband has so many enemies and is defenseless. She has just learned that King was attacked by a white racist in Birmingham and did not defend himself. He refused to press charges saying, "The system we live under creates people such as this youth. I'm interested in changing the kind of system that produces such men."

Above: *King thought of himself as a family man and treasured the times he had with his wife and children. His demanding schedule kept him away from home almost half the week. King's absence made Coretta almost entirely responsible for raising the family. At this time the Kings are expecting their fourth child, Bernice, whom they called Bunny.*

Right: *An elated King tosses his daughter Bunny into the air. He had recently learned that he had won the Nobel Peace Prize.*

Opposite: *The King family enjoys a rare musical moment at home. Coretta King, a graduate of the New England Conservatory of Music, reluctantly gave up a career in music when she married and moved back to the South.*

Newspapers under his arm, King returns home with his son Marty. Although in college King had been a sharp dresser, by this time in his life, for spiritual reasons, he dressed carefully and conservatively in less expensive suits.

the lagging standards which are the effects of segregation. There must be a rhythm of alteration between attacking the cause and healing the effects."

Some blacks were critical of King for those observations, although he was only being true to his first calling, that of a Baptist minister (often he dreamed of one day teaching theology at a college), and to his own words in his inspiring sermon "Transformed Nonconformist," in which he wrote, "Any Christian who blindly accepts the opinions of the majority and in fear and timidity follows a path of expediency and social approval is a mental and spiritual slave."

A portrait of Mohandas Gandhi, King's idol, hangs in a place of honor in the Kings' home.

The King family relaxes together at home in 1963.

King's office at the SCLC was so small that he often met with his staff in a local restaurant.

King and, to his right, his aide James Bevel, and others join together for a strategy meeting in summer 1966. At this time Bevel was instrumental in involving King in the peace movement.

Opposite, top: *King, who devoted much of his life to black suffrage, casts his vote while Coretta waits her turn. In King's view, voting was the key to black liberation. As the country's leading spokesman for the black community, King was always courted by politicians.*

Opposite, bottom: *King talks to a reporter as he marches in a picket line at the Scripto plant. The picketers are demanding equal pay for black workers.*

Left: *In October 1960, an officer escorts King to court after he takes part in a student sit-in demonstration at Rich's, an Atlanta department store.*

Below: *On December 13, 1963, police surround King, protecting him at an anti-segregation rally. They were equally likely to arrest him at such demonstrations. Here he addresses more than two thousand people gathered in Atlanta's Hurt Park in freezing weather.*

Opposite: *An electrifying preacher, King commiserated with his congregation and dramatized his own struggles, yet he always educated, exhorted, and exalted. He often returned to Atlanta from movement campaigns to join his parishioners on Sunday.*

Above: *King and his father, co-pastors of Atlanta's Ebenezer Baptist Church, sit side by side. Moving back to Atlanta, where he could share the pulpit and pastoral duties with his father, gave King more time to devote to his family and the battle for equality.*

Left: *Rev. King chats with a parishioner after Sunday services. Friends and staff marveled that King was always thoughtful and attentive to everyone he dealt with, treating them in the most respectful and amiable way.*

The Greyhound bus carrying Freedom Riders from Washington, D.C., to New Orleans is attacked by a mob outside Anniston, Alabama.

FREEDOM RIDES
Days and nights of mayhem

Freedom Riders must develop the quiet courage of dying for a cause.

Martin Luther King, Jr.,
at a nonviolent training session

The next great chapter in the fight for freedom belonged to the students. On February 1, 1960, Joseph McNeill, a student at North Carolina Agricultural and Technical College, his roommate Ezell Blair, Jr., and two other students sat down at a segregated Woolworth's lunch counter in Greensboro, North Carolina, for service. Predictably, they were told Negroes could not eat there, so they returned day after day with the same demand, which inspired students across North Carolina to do the same in other public establishments, like dominoes falling, until fifty cities in the South witnessed increasingly militant young people (inspired by King, but acting spontaneously on their own) defying racial inequality and packing the nation's jails. By April this sit-in movement found its own organizational apparatus, the Student Nonviolent Coordinating Committee (SNCC).

These students identified with their counterparts in Africa, the Far East, and South America, who were taking to the streets to defy colonialism. And the violence they endured, the humiliations, and the denials of their humanity by vicious white supremacists enraged all Americans of goodwill, none more so than King himself, who in October delivered a speech to inspire SNCC activists, and then with thirty-six others was thrown in jail after they demanded to be served at a lunch counter in Rich's, a department store in Atlanta.

King refused to post bail. Five or six days later, trespassing charges were dropped by the merchants, and all were released—except King. He was served papers stating that he'd violated his probation for a traffic offense earlier in May. (When moving from Montgomery back to Atlanta, he'd neglected to change his state driver's license.) Then he was taken, chained like a hardened criminal, to Reidsville state prison. Only through the intervention of a furious Robert Kennedy, then campaign manager for his brother John's presidential campaign, who called Georgia's governor and Judge J. Oscar Mitchell (while his brother John, only weeks away from the November elections, consoled a pregnant Coretta by phone), was King's incarceration in a segregated cell block, reserved for the worst offenders, limited to an overnight stay.

But the offensive phase of the civil rights movement had only just begun. On May 4, 1961, the Congress of Racial Equality (CORE), an interracial, nonviolent, passivist organization founded in 1942 in Chicago, initiated a project called the Freedom Rides. In Washington, D.C., they placed two groups of twelve activists and a CORE observer on Trailways and Greyhound buses, directing them to test throughout the Deep South the Supreme Court's ruling to desegregate buses and terminals. In Rock Hill, South Carolina, they were assaulted; in Winnsboro, South Carolina, they were arrested. Near Anniston, Alabama, one of the buses was attacked by a white mob that broke windows, slashed tires, hurled a bomb that set the vehicle on fire, then beat the Freedom Riders as they emerged, trying to escape the flames. Although rescued by Rev. Fred Shuttlesworth and his group, the Alabama Christian Movement for Human Rights, they were too injured to continue the ride. The second bus, traveling to Birmingham, was also greeted by whites, who assaulted them with lead pipes, baseball bats, and bicycle chains with the consent of the police, who watched passively for fifteen minutes. Yet not once did the Freedom Riders retaliate with violence. At this point in their hellish odyssey, the bus companies refused to take them any farther. SNCC activists in Nashville picked up the torch, continuing the ride into Montgomery, where on May 20 they too were mobbed for twenty minutes by hundreds of whites, some of them Ku Klux Klan members. James Zwerg, a white student from Fisk University, was the first to step off the bus and was mauled.

The MIA sheltered the Riders in Rev. Abernathy's First Baptist Church. King traveled to Montgomery and spoke to twelve hundred people in the church. As the congregation sang

While the Freedom Riders are being viciously attacked in Montgomery, a news photographer is knocked to the ground and kicked, and his equipment spills out of his bag. Why attack a photographer? A picture is evidence.

"We Shall Overcome," several thousand whites surrounded the church. A car was set on fire. Then rocks crashed through First Baptist's stained-glass windows, raining splintered glass onto those gathered inside. From the church basement King called Robert Kennedy, who assured him that close to seven hundred U.S. marshals had already been dispatched. So they huddled together in a church under siege. They heard fighting outside. Then at last the federal government forced Governor John Patterson to call in the National Guard, which enabled those trapped in the church to go home and the Freedom Riders to continue their dangerous and historic journey on to Jackson, Mississippi, their battered bus protected by three airplanes, two helicopters, and seven patrol cars.

King was criticized by Riders who begged him to join them on the trip from Montgomery to Jackson. Given that he was on probation, he declined, which did not please some who reboarded the bus. Still, the Freedom Rides continued, taking the civil rights movement toward an unprecedented level of mass demonstrations. Three hundred more would be arrested in Jackson before the rides ended. But their heroism, and the crisis into which the country had been plunged by Jim Crow, led that September to the Interstate Commerce Commission's outlawing segregation in interstate buses and terminals. While King generally took a secondary, supportive role during the Freedom Rides and sit-ins, he served as chairman for the Freedom Rider Coordinating Committee, which provided workshops in nonviolent civil disobedience, and he praised their achievements time and again. Yet he was concerned that many young activists saw nonviolence only as a tactic, not as a way of life. He reminded them that "resistance and nonviolence are not in themselves good. There is another element that must be present in our struggle that then makes our resistance and nonviolence truly meaningful. That element is reconciliation. Our ultimate end must be the creation of the beloved community."

In a culminating event on that fateful May 20th, more than a thousand congregants at Rev. Abernathy's First Baptist Church in Montgomery welcomed the Freedome Riders into their midst, but all became trapped when an angry white mob gathered outside. On the opposite page we see the worried, frustrated, and fearful leaders Abernathy and King, and then King trying to bolster those in the church: "Fear not, we've come too far to turn back." At right, as the seige wore on, some of the exhausted slept in the pews.

Opposite, top: *On Monday King and bandaged Freedom Rider John Lewis hold a news conference in Montgomery to tell the press that the Freedom Riders will continue on to Jackson, Mississippi.*

Opposite, bottom: *The Riders are disappointed with King's decision not to join them. He explains that he is on probation and that an arrest would violate it.*

Here, King shakes hands and bids them a safe journey.

Freedom Rider Dave Dennis, glances warily at the National Guardsmen. The Riders reached Mississippi's capital without incident. Once off the bus, they were arrested.

ALBANY
A painful lesson for the movement

On December 16, 1961, swept up in the high spirits of the Albany
Movement, King leads a spur-of-the-moment demonstration to
City Hall, where he and his followers are stopped and arrested by
his canny adversary, Police Chief Laurie Pritchett.

Above: *Pritchett arrests King in front of City Hall on a charge of parading without a permit, and then King, in this picture, sits pensively in the police chief's office after his arrest.*

ALBANY

A painful lesson for the movement

*We should not devour each other to the delight of onlookers
who would have us corrupt and sully the noble quality of our crusade.*

Martin Luther King, Jr., Albany, 1961

Albany, Georgia, was a dangerous cauldron of contradictions. King only went to give a speech. Why get involved, he must have wondered, when SNCC already was battling in Albany for voting rights and the desegregation of public facilities. And besides, they feared his presence would overshadow the local leadership. But he went, invited by physician William G. Anderson, who defied SNCC's refusal to bring on board the celebrated, idealistic theist

Above: *Singing a medley of songs including "I Woke Up This Morning with My Mind Set on Freedom, Hallelujah!," picketers carry placards protesting the arrest of demonstrators for exercising their First Amendment right to peaceful assembly.*

Left: *After a night of violence, King visits Albany, Georgia's "Harlem," stopping at a pool hall. "I hate to hold up your game. I used to be a pool shark myself." He then tried to enlist the crowd to join the effort to end segregation nonviolently.*

King's oratory mightily stirs Albany blacks, who fill a church to overflowing. He discusses the difficulties they will face as they try to upset a federal injunction forbidding demonstrations, which he has decided to obey. A higher court removed the injunction, but by that time violence had broken out, and King limited his activities to prayer vigils as he tried to avoid more violence.

Clergymen from the north who journeyed to Albany to aid his work surround King at an integration rally held on August 28, 1962.

from Atlanta. And when 31-year-old King saw the passion and commitment of the black people packing Shiloh Baptist Church on December 15, 1961, he was moved and felt that perhaps Albany would provide his first major campaign since the bus boycott in Montgomery.

Sadly, it delivered King's first stinging defeat: a cornucopia of realpolitik. Despite the broad range of confrontational tactics employed by the SCLC on its maiden campaign, no more than 5 percent of Albany's black population (which was nearly half of the city) turned out for a bus boycott, nonviolence workshops, mass meetings, and sit-ins at the Jim Crow library and recreational facilities. Worse, King discovered blacks willing to work with the segregationists to maintain the status quo if they could personally profit from doing so.

Furthermore, after he, Abernathy, and other demonstrators were arrested at the bus station by Police Chief Laurie Pritchett for disturbing the peace and parading without a permit, King vowed to be in jail through Christmas. But information he received while in jail led him to believe the Albany officials had blinked, agreeing to a truce. His bail was posted. He emerged hoping to see jubilant protesters but discovered that the local leadership, suspicious of him, had terminated the demonstrations in exchange for the city's promise to consider its demands. Yet Albany was as segregated as it had been before. Embarrassed, King apologized profusely for leaving jail prematurely.

King and the SCLC renewed their efforts, but they seriously underestimated Chief Pritchett, who had taken the time to study King's Gandhian strategies. He was an adversary they came to respect, for, like the city officials, Pritchett was a cunning player of the chess game known as nonviolent civil disobedience. Did the movement rely on publicity? Melodramatic footage of good Negroes being savaged by evil, Neanderthal whites? Well then, Pritchett decided, during the Albany demonstrations his policemen would be the very portrait of restraint and respect before the world's cameras; he even bowed his head when demonstrators prayed, then he politely arrested them. Ironically, it was like fighting fire with fire, countering the protesters' lawfulness with public civility and compassion by the police. Would King symbolize the frustration of Negroes if he were jailed? In Albany, white segregationists enlisted a Negro to pay their fines. SCLC leaders were perplexed. "I've been thrown out of a lot of places in my day," Abernathy said, "but never before have I been thrown out of a jail."

Pritchett assigned 24-hour police protection for King, another zugzwang that annoyed King no end. Officers arrested demonstrators left and right, but without a shred of recordable abuse—that took place only outside the city, for example at a prison where a pregnant woman was kicked so severely she later lost her child.

The SCLC found Albany to be a tissue of frustrations. They could not find enough protesters to fill the jails. Local leaders criticized their every move. On July 24, young blacks hurled rocks and bottles at the police, shattering King's insistence on nonviolence. That led to the city's calling in the National Guard, to King's pleading in pool halls with the black population to be nonviolent, and to declaring "A Day of Penance." The bus company agreed to desegregate, then shut down business altogether. The city parks were closed. So too the public library. And the federal government offered no help whatsoever, not even to enforce the law. Indeed, Robert Kennedy recommended that King conclude his operations in Albany.

Militant students dismissed King's "Day of Penance" as weak, his methods as timid and riddled with poor judgment, and his performance as disappointing. The coup de grâce came in the form of a temporary injunction against civil disobedience in Albany. (In August the Justice Department would challenge this, but too late to undo the damage.) Because he did not wish to oppose the federal courts, which had helped the movement in the past, King obeyed the injunction. Local leaders and those in SNCC condemned him for that decision.

In the end, a disappointed King and the SCLC achieved none of their desegregation goals in Albany. They had entered that campaign with a vague purpose. Without a plan. Without knowledge of the local situation and its intra-movement factionalism. They were fed misinformation and checkmated at virtually every stage of the game. The civil rights movement, the burgeoning struggle for black liberation was not, King saw, in his control. But from this lost battle he and the fledgling SCLC learned much that would prove useful in future campaigns.

BIRMINGHAM
Segregation is brought to its knees

We will wear you down by our capacity to suffer.

> Martin Luther King, Jr.,
> Birmingham, 1963

Bull Connor has done as much for civil rights as Abraham Lincoln.

> President John F. Kennedy, 1963

If Albany had been chaos, Birmingham was a magnificent symphony of brilliant strategies and sacrifices that forever changed America. King and the SCLC planned this campaign, "Project C" (Confrontation) as they called it, with veteran freedom fighter Rev. Fred Shuttlesworth months in advance. They studied and anticipated the actions of their adversaries—racist Police Commissioner Eugene "Bull" Connor and Alabama Governor George Wallace—and others in what was considered to be this nation's most segregated and brutally repressive city. Knowing their phones were tapped, they devised code words. (Jail was "going to get baptized.") Twice they postponed Project C, first in order to monitor the elections for mayor in Birmingham, then to wait for the outcome of Connor's runoff election against Albert Boutwell, who won. (Shuttlesworth called Boutwell "just a dignified Bull Connor.") The very next day, April 3, 1963, Project C was launched, although the delays had reduced the number of volunteers determined to go to jail from two hundred fifty to sixty-five.

From the start the Birmingham campaign was focused. It targeted not the political power structure but segregated businesses—Woolworth's, H. L. Green's, and J. J. Newberry's—and produced a manifesto that demanded desegregation of all public facilities in stores, hiring of blacks by employers, the formation of a biracial committee to expedite integration, dismissal of all charges from previous protests, equal opportunity for blacks within the city government, and the reopening of closed municipal facilities on a desegregated basis. The SCLC and Shuttlesworth's Alabama Christian Movement for Human Rights began cautiously to conserve their resources and gradually build a crisis that would crescendo by Easter. They initially fielded only a few sit-ins, and Birmingham's divided government (split because the three city commissioners, Connor among them, declared they would remain in office until 1965) responded predictably by imitating strategies employed in Albany. Connor ordered his police officers to behave amicably. Then a court injunction was obtained, ordering the demonstrators to stop.

This time, however—and for the first time—King decided to disobey a court order. Wearing denim work clothes similar to those of Alabama's poor, he marched toward downtown Birmingham with Ralph Abernathy on Good Friday, April 12, and after only eight blocks they were arrested. King was thrown into solitary confinement.

It was there, in a darkened cell, without a single note or textbook to refer to, and after he read a statement by eight Christian and Jewish clergy condemning his actions in the *Birmingham News,* that King composed, first in the margins of that paper, then on toilet paper, and finally on a legal pad provided by his lawyers, the philosophically and morally breathtaking "Letter from Birmingham Jail," destined to become one of the great political documents in American history. "Any law that uplifts human personality is just," he wrote. "Any law that degrades human personality is unjust."

Upon his release, secured by $50,000 in bail funds raised by Harry Belafonte and the intervention of the Kennedys, King turned up the heat under the demonstrations, which had

Before the campaign begins, King addresses a mass rally at the Sixteenth Street Baptist Church, headquarters for the protest. Once the demonstrations started, mass meetings were held nightly.

King's truly exalted oratory had to persuade his followers not only to believe in his vision but also to act on it. By faith and by deed, armed only with Christian love and non-violent acts, they could overturn a vicious, cruel, and oppressive caste system. Birmingham would test the strength of his vision and both his and the people's courage.

Speaking at an organizing rally, King calls on those joining the protest to wear overalls until Easter to show their solidarity with the people boycotting Birmingham's segregated stores.

dwindled. They needed an army to fill the city's jails. Where to find it? The SCLC looked toward the high-school students they had trained in nonviolence and discovered that hundreds of their younger siblings in the elementary schools insisted on fighting for freedom too. Thus was born the controversial "children's crusade" that put one thousand youngsters on Birmingham's streets. The next day the number reached twenty-five hundred and Bull Connor responded with fire hoses. An angry crowd of fifteen hundred reacted violently to the treatment of the children. Connor then used police dogs—a show of brutality that in news footage broadcast worldwide sickened America and people everywhere.

It sickened the firemen, too. On May 5, hundreds of blacks held a prayer meeting near the city jail. When Connor shouted, "Dammit! Turn on the hoses," his men fell back as if they were mesmerized, some weeping, and let them proceed. King's masterful plan to "create such a crisis and foster such a tension in a community which has constantly refused to negotiate" had worked. The businessmen of Birmingham reached an agreement on King's manifesto on May 10. For the first time in the movement's history, jails had been filled. Out of the agony of the Birmingham campaign, a broad-based coalition involving the NAACP Legal Defense Fund, the United Automobile Workers, and diverse groups dedicated to liberty and reform was forged. Added to which President Kennedy pressed the very next month for passage of a civil rights bill.

Tragically, the racist backlash continued in Birmingham after the settlement. The home of King's brother, A. D., and King's room at the Gaston Motel were bombed on May 11, probably by Klansmen. Blacks responded in kind, burning and looting and attacking the police. Finally, Kennedy dispatched three thousand federal troops to a location just outside Birmingham and promised to federalize the Alabama National Guard in order to quell the rioting on both sides and safeguard the settlement.

Like all of King's campaigns thus far, violence followed close on the heels of nonviolent civil disobedience. But Birmingham had proven to be a turning point for the movement (and the world), one that no segregationist—whether he resided in the governor's mansion or hid beneath a white robe—could reverse.

After his April 12 arrest, King stayed in jail, where he wrote his famous "Letter from Birmingham Jail" defending the demonstrations.

King stages nightly mass meetings, at which he exhorts his followers to victory through love and nonviolence.

Scenes that shook the world: here the Children's Crusade, while below and opposite, we see Bull Connor's hoses and his dogs. The bottom photograph opposite shows a downed onlooker rising up, enraged at the firemen.

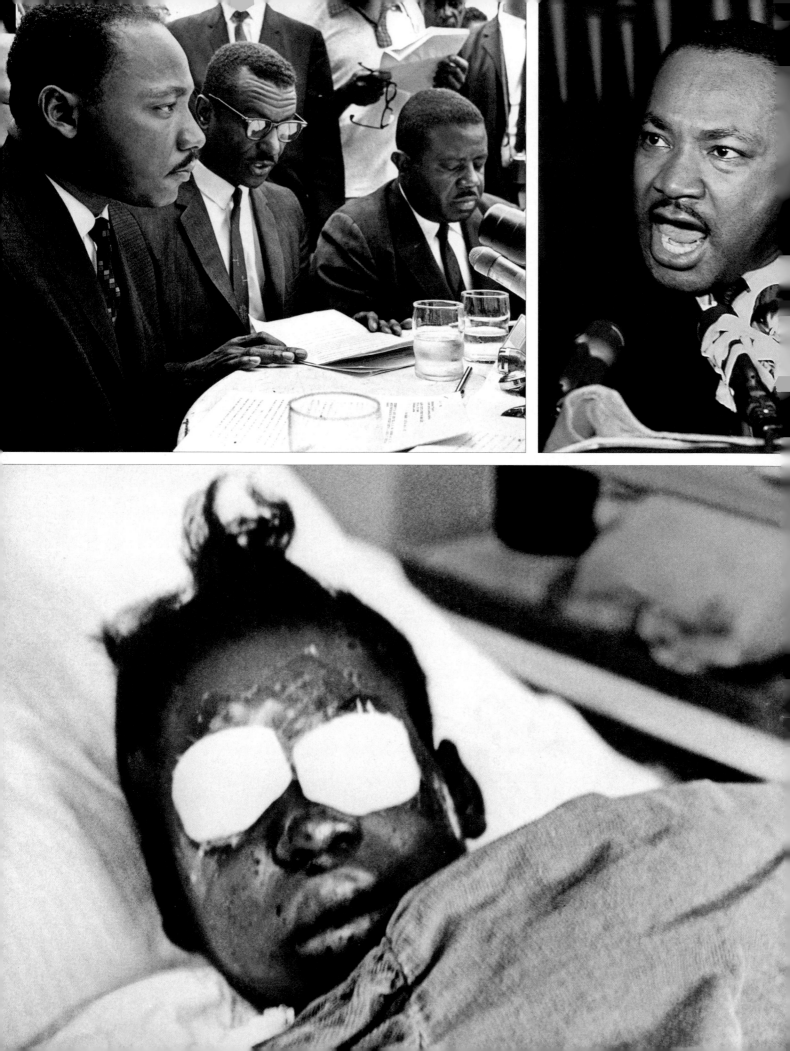

King at two Birmingham press conferences, opposite above. On the left, the settlement that has been mediated to end segregation and provide jobs in Birmingham's stores is announced. At right, only a few months later, a furious King rages in response to the September 15, 1963 bombing of the Sixteenth Street Baptist Church, in which four children attending Sunday School were killed. In the picture below, Sarah Jean Collins, whose sister was one of the murdered, was struck in the eyes by flying glass; she was one of twenty injured. Here, King, Abernathy, and Shuttlesworth enter church to mourn the innocent victims. King will end his eulogy, "Goodnight sweet princesses; may the flight of angels take thee to thy eternal rest."

Marchers gathered at the Washington Monument on August 28, 1963, and marched to the Lincoln Memorial. The march is led by King, fresh from his momentous victory in Birmingham, hand in hand with Floyd McKissick of CORE on his right and arm in arm with a clergyman on his left.

MARCH ON WASHINGTON
The dreamer elevates the nation

I have a dream my four little children will one day live in a nation where they will not be judged by the color of their skin but by the content of their character. I have a dream today!

Martin Luther King, Jr.,
Washington, D.C., August 28, 1963

In the centennial year of the Emancipation Proclamation, just three months after the decisive Birmingham campaign, two months after the murder of NAACP leader Medgar Evers, and a scant three months before John F. Kennedy's assassination, a quarter of a million Americans—black and white and from across the full spectrum of progressive organizations—traveled to participate in the monumental March on Washington for jobs and freedom. While the nonviolent, orderly march would add even more credibility to King's philosophical position, he, with his characteristic generosity and humility, saw it not as a platform for himself but rather as the fulfillment of a long-held dream of A. Philip Randolph, the dean of America's black leaders, who in 1941 and 1947 had hoped to realize a similar event. Now Randolph met with representatives from all the civil rights organizations, and with Walter Reuther, president of the United Auto Workers, to prepare a protest march of staggering yet inspiring proportions that would speed Kennedy's Civil Rights Bill through Congress. Bayard Rustin served as the march's national organizer. King's speech, scheduled as the final, keynote address, was to be limited to eight minutes, like all the others.

In Washington, D.C., at the Willard Hotel, King spent all night before the march working on his words, doubtful he would be able to express in eight minutes all that needed to be said. Perhaps, he thought, he could resurrect the refrain "I have a dream" he'd used so often before, most recently at Detroit's Cobo Hall in June. So far so good. But his presentation needed to thematically reach back one hundred years to revitalize Abraham Lincoln's call in the Gettysburg Address to reaffirm the equality of all men. After an hour of reflection, King settled on the simple, straightforward metaphor of America having issued blacks a bad check in respect to the "promissory note" signed by the Founders that said all men would be guaranteed the unalienable rights of "life, liberty, and the pursuit of happiness." He asked close

Below: The ceremony commences on the steps of the Lincoln Memorial, King stands between Whitney Young, Jr., of the Urban League, and Walter Reuther, president of the United Auto Workers as they salute the flag. Then, here, he steps to the podium. To a rising crescendo of cheers and applause, King delivers the most memorable speech of his life, climaxing in the moment seen on the following spread: He raises his arm and calls out for deliverance with the electrifying words from an old spiritual, "Free at last! Free at last! Thank God almighty, we are free at last!"

At left, the audience at the largest mass-protest meeting in the nation's history strains to hear and enthusiastically responds to King's inspiring words. Also listening intently is an honored guest, Rosa Parks, above.

friends—Ralph Abernathy, Andrew Young, and Walter Fauntroy—for their reactions, and by four in the morning on August 28, King was done, or so he thought.

Initially, the march organizers feared a low turnout, and they hoped attendance would reach at least one hundred thousand. By noon their fears were dispelled when they saw crowds surging at the base of the Washington Monument. Whites had shown up in record numbers for the first time in movement history. And, unlike in Birmingham, white men of the cloth came, too, demonstrating their commitment to racial justice. Not only was this becoming the largest march ever assembled in the nation's capital, it was also a phenomenal media event, with people such as Mahalia Jackson, Joan Baez, Sidney Poitier, Charlton Heston, Harry Belafonte, Marlon Brando, Burt Lancaster, and Bob Dylan on hand to entertain the demonstrators and millions of Americans who watched the well-orchestrated proceedings on television.

And what did they see? For King, they witnessed a devastating denial of black stereotypes. A public relations coup. They saw impressive, learned black spokesmen ("If the press had expected something akin to a minstrel show," King observed later, "or a brawl, or a comic display of odd clothes and bad manners, they were disappointed") who embodied the finest American ideals and levels of cultural achievement. All were a credit to the (human) race. (Indeed, white Americans would not see on their televisions another collective representation of real black professionalism and distinction such as this until the Supreme Court confirmation hearings for Clarence Thomas decades later.)

Camilla Williams began the ceremony at one-thirty, with a spirited rendition of "The Star-Spangled Banner." The speakers and entertainers came next, one after another, the crowd attentive until mid-afternoon, then beginning to thin around three o'clock when Roy Wilkins appeared at the podium. Some left. Those who remained were rejuvenated by Mahalia Jack-

Civil rights and labor leaders are greeted by President Kennedy at the successful conclusion of the march. The president congratulated King on his speech and told his aides how much he was impressed by it. When he greeted King, Kennedy said, "I have a dream," which embarrassed King because he was singled out among the many who had spoken.

son's moving delivery of "I Been 'Buked and I Been Scorned," and when she was done Randolph introduced King, the last speaker, as "the moral leader of the nation." He began with the speech he had finished just hours before, then, as so often happened with King, he began to feel the energy of his audience, their clapping and shouting, which fed his spirit so fully he turned away from his prepared text and launched extemporaneously into the words that would echo for decades in the ears of the American people:

"And when we allow freedom to ring...we will be able to speed up that day when all of God's children...will be able to join hands and sing in the words of the old Negro spiritual, 'Free at last! Free at last! Thank God almighty, we are free at last!'"

For Martin Luther King, Jr., newly anointed as the powerful voice of America's moral conscience, and for the nation as a whole, the March on Washington and his "I Have a Dream" speech lifted the civil rights movement as well as Western humanism to undreamed of and dizzying new heights.

One of the march's aims was realized the following year, when President Lyndon Johnson signed into law the 1964 Civil Rights Act. He shakes the hand of the man who led the charge to outlaw segregation.

NOBEL PRIZE

A pacifist shares his glory

King and his wife, Coretta, celebrate the news that he has received the 1964 Nobel Peace Prize. King was in a hospital in Atlanta recovering from fatigue and illness brought on by his travel and work for the movement. Sharing the honor, King said, "This Nobel Prize was won by a movement of great people whose discipline, wise restraint, and majestic courage has led them down a nonviolent course in seeking to establish a reign of justice and a rule of love across this nation of ours."

Civilization and violence are antithetical concepts.

Martin Luther King, Jr.,
Nobel Prize acceptance speech, 1964

He was in Atlanta's St. Joseph's Hospital, exhausted and badly in need of rest, when his wife telephoned at 9 a.m. to relay the news: He had won the Nobel Peace Prize. At first King was disbelieving and felt like a man in a dream, yet it was so. At thirty-five he was suddenly, that October morning in 1964, the youngest Nobel laureate to receive the world's most coveted award and only the third black, following Ralph Bunche and South Africa's Chief Albert Luthuli. Where the Civil Rights Act only a few months earlier was vindication for the efforts of thousands of civil rights activists, this honor—which truly thrust King onto the world stage—was the ultimate acknowledgment of his vision of agapic love, social interdependence, and the beloved community. But King, of course, would never claim it for himself alone. It was, he said, for the nameless "ground crew" of activists who would never appear in Who's Who but upon whose shoulders he stood. And the $54,600 prize money? That he decided to donate to the SCLC, CORE, SNCC, the NAACP, the National Council of Negro Women, and the American Foundation for Nonviolence.

King and his entourage left for the ceremony in Norway on December 4. They stopped in London, where King delivered his sermon "The Three Dimensions of a Complete Life" at St. Paul's Cathedral. He reminded his audience of four thousand that the first dimension was self-acceptance, development of one's personal resources, and doing life's work "so well that the living, the dead, or the unborn couldn't do it any better"; the second service to mankind was learning "that there is nothing greater than to do something for others"; and the third, said King, was the quest for the divine, for "We were made for God, and we will be restless until we find rest in him."

Stopping off in Stockholm to join the other Nobel laureates after receiving his Peace Prize in Oslo, King is treated to a traditional breakfast celebrating the Feast of St. Lucia, the Festival of Lights, which begins the Swedish Christmas season.

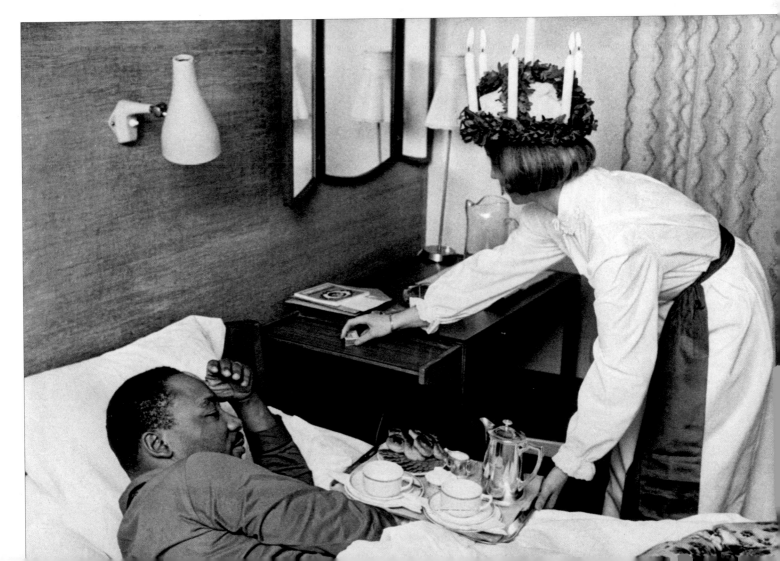

From London, King traveled on to Oslo, where he was met on December 8 by Nobel officials, an excited crowd of young people, and children who showered bouquets of flowers upon him, his family, and his friends. And the press was after him now in a new way, asking him questions about world affairs, for as a Nobel laureate his views were indisputably of global significance.

For the ceremony in Aula Hall at Oslo University, King dressed in striped trousers, a gray tailcoat, and an ascot (which he very much disliked). He was introduced by the chairman of the Norwegian Parliament as "the first person in the Western world to have shown us that a struggle can be waged without violence." (The unstated implication of Gandhi's nonviolent approach in the Eastern world is interesting to note insofar as King, later, would nominate for the Nobel Peace Prize Thich Nhat Hahn, the poet, outstanding Buddhist teacher, and chairman of the Vietnam Peace Delegation. Of King, Nhat Hahn says in his book *Living Buddha, Living Christ*, "The moment I met Martin Luther King, Jr., I knew I was in the presence of a holy person. Not just his good work but his very being was a source of great inspiration for me." That friendship with Nhat Hahn, which began in 1966, contributed to King's opposition to the Vietnam War.)

The following day King formally accepted his prize "in the spirit of the curator of some precious heirloom which he holds in trust for its true owners—all those to whom beauty is truth and truth beauty—and in whose eyes the beauty of genuine brotherhood and peace is more precious than diamonds or silver or gold." He continued, speaking what were perhaps the most profound words of his career:

"Nonviolence is the answer to the crucial political and moral questions of our time.…The foundation of such a method is love.…I have the audacity to believe that peoples everywhere can have three meals a day for their bodies, education and culture for their minds, and dignity, equality and freedom for their spirits."

Yes, indeed, in Oslo King had at last arrived on the mountaintop. In Stockholm he attended a reception for all the Nobel winners that year—and he noted as he traveled through Norway how well a democratic, socialist country provided universal heath care and free education for its people. Although tired during the trip back through Paris, and taking sleeping pills, when he arrived in New York fireboats on the Hudson River geysered fountains of water to welcome him home and the mayor presented him with the Medallion of Honor. On and on that December he moved through celebratory festivities—at the White House, in the home of New York's Governor Nelson Rockefeller, to the streets of Baltimore, and to Atlanta. To the people of Harlem, filling a black church in his honor, he said, "I really wish I could just stay on the mountain, but I must go back to the valley. I must go back because my brothers and sisters down in Mississippi and Alabama can't register and vote."

That valley had a name: Selma.

And there, far from the heights, King would descend yet again into the hell of America's racial nightmare.

Dr. Martin Luther King, Jr., above left, receives the Nobel Peace Prize from Gunnar Jahn, chairman of the Nobel Committee, at Oslo University on December 10, 1964. King proudly accepts it, saying, "I still believe that one day mankind will bow down before the altars of God and be crowned triumphant over war and bloodshed, and nonviolent redemptive goodwill will proclaim the rule of the land. I still believe that we shall overcome." In his laureate's speech, above, King pleads for brotherly love and for the use of nonviolent means to resolve conflicts. In the photograph opposite, he quietly regards the medallion.

SELMA

The law of the land written in blood

*We must come to see that the end we seek is a society at peace with itself,
a society that can live with its conscience. That will be a day not of the white man,
not of the black man. That will be the day of man as man.*

Martin Luther King, Jr.,
Selma, 1965

Showing initial restraint, Sheriff Jim Clark denies King, Abernathy, and local residents access to the Dallas County Courthouse in Selma, where they have come to attempt to register to vote

Less than sixty days after King received the Nobel Peace Prize, he was in jail again, immersed in Project Alabama, which had two primary objectives: first, to accelerate voter registration for the 70 percent of blacks who lacked the franchise in five states of the Deep South; and second, to convince Lyndon Baines Johnson that voting rights legislation was needed. The president was sympathetic, but doubted Congress would approve a new bill for blacks so soon after the passage of the Civil Rights Act the previous year, and he told King he needed the support of the southern bloc for other Great Society programs.

King knew what he had to do, where, and how. Like Birmingham, Selma provided a perfect stage for his organizational genius. It offered the possibilities of spectacle. It provided hissable villains—segregationist governor George Wallace and atavistic white supremacists led by Sheriff Jim Clark (a clone of "Bull" Connor), who arrested blacks for meeting together (a violation of their First Amendment rights). Sadly, there would be martyrs too, three in all. And, as with any masterfully constructed drama, the denouement would be more far reaching and greater than the sum of its players, surprising even King himself in its plot twists, cameos, and subplots.

"We will bring a voting bill into being on the streets of Selma," King had vowed. The battle begins. King and Abernathy and their followers kneel in prayer on February 1, 1965. At that time, only 1 percent of the blacks in Selma were registered although they made up half of the population.

King stands in front of the Hotel Albert, where he was to successfully register for a room, testing the hotel's compliance with the 1964 Civil Rights Act barring segregated public facilities. His checking-in was not without incident, however. Earlier, a man named Jimmy Robinson, a member of the racist National States Rights Party, had confronted King during a courthouse protest (opposite, top left). Now, seeing King and his colleagues registering at the hotel's front desk (opposite, top right), Robinson savagely attacks King from behind (opposite, bottom).

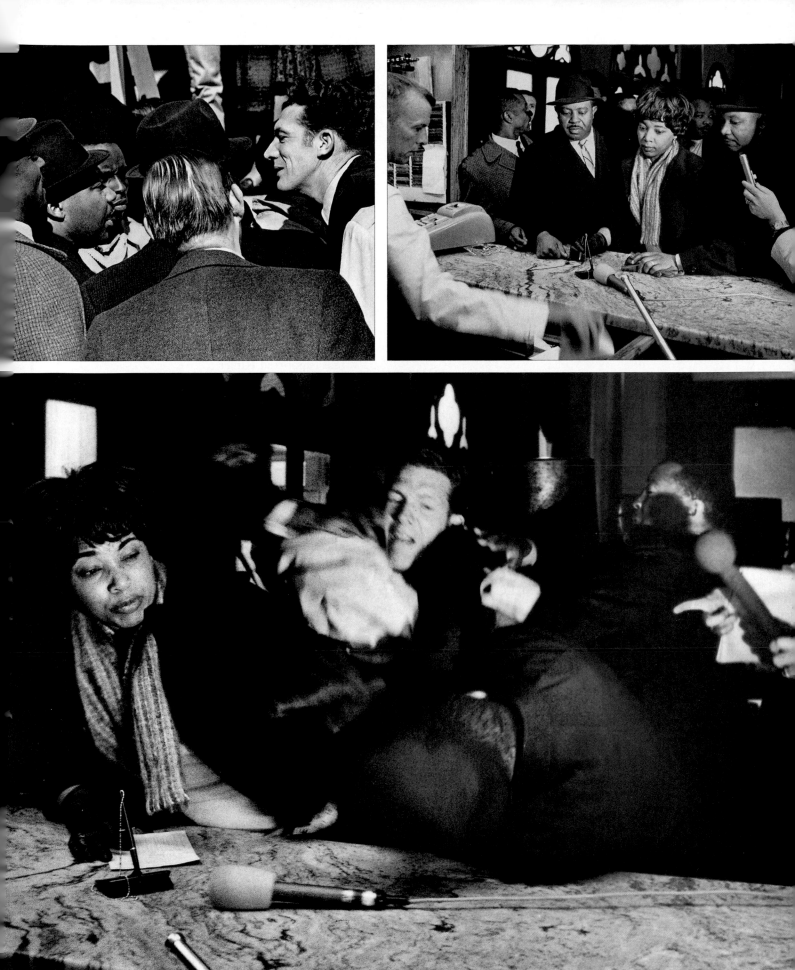

An unshaven King meets with colleagues after he is released from jail. The escalation of confrontations and the jailings, along with King's many responsibilities, visibly strain him.

Reeb, none to Jackson's family—a racial slight that was not lost on the increasingly militant SNCC.) Johnson told Congress he would put a voting rights act on the fast track, the front burner, stating, "What happened in Selma is part of a far larger movement which reaches into every section and state of America. It is the effort of American Negroes to secure for themselves the full blessings of American life....Their cause must be our cause, too. Because it is not just Negroes...who must overcome the crippling legacy of bigotry and injustice. And we shall overcome."

Thus did the curtain rise on a majestic Act Three unparalleled in American political history. More good news came when a Montgomery judge green-lighted the fifty-four-mile Selma to Montgomery march. Protected by a federalized Alabama National Guard and four thousand Army troops provided by the president, King and five thousand marchers who cut across all divisions of religion, race, and class began their historic trek on Sunday, March 21. They slept in tents, tramped down the Jefferson Davis Highway through the rain, and passed billboards splashed with photos of King supposedly at a "Communist training camp" (in fact, it was a racially mixed, civil rights and union organizer workshop at Highlander Folk School in Tennessee), and on Wednesday they reached Montgomery, where ten years earlier the civil rights movement had begun with a bus boycott. That night marchers and others arriving from all over the country were entertained by performers as diverse as Leonard Bernstein, Harry Belafonte, Sammy Davis, Jr., Billy Eckstine, and Peter, Paul, and Mary, to name only a few.

On Thursday, March 25, King, at the head of twenty-five thousand people, delivered the petition of Selma's black people for voting rights and the end of fascist police treatment. Wallace refused to accept it. He stayed in the capitol building and sulked, looking through his window at thousands of Americans who had taken a stand for brotherhood and smashed the last century-old obstacle to black equality. For many, this was—and remains—the movement's, and King's, finest hour.

King steps over a puddle as he leads yet another column of marchers to the courthouse to attempt to register to vote.

On March 7, 1965, more than five hundred marchers led by John Lewis and Hosea Williams crossed the Edmund Pettus Bridge as they set off for Montgomery. When they reached the other side, Alabama State Police barred their way and ordered them to disperse within two minutes. Seconds after the order, even though the marchers began to retreat, state police rushed the marchers, gassing and brutally clubbing them to the ground. Above, a victim is aided. At least seventy protesters required treatment for broken bones and head wounds. The police expected to frighten and intimidate them and end the demonstrations. The vicious attack, now known as Bloody Sunday, was filmed and photographed, then seen by an appalled nation, making passage of a voting rights act a near certainty.

Awaiting court approval of the march to Montgomery, protestors and the police regularly faced off a few hundred feet from Brown's Chapel. The police blockade was variously called "the Selma wall" and "the 38th parallel" by the protestors.

King was profoundly shaken by Bloody Sunday, distraught that he hadn't been there to bear witness. He then meets in Montgomery with other civil rights leaders to plan strategy for the ongoing campaign.

Eulogizing the martyrs: King at the services for, here, Jimmy Lee Jackson and, opposite, Rev. James Reeb, where he said Reeb was "murdered by an atmosphere of inhumanity in Alabama that tolerated the vicious murder of Jimmy Lee Jackson in Marion and the brutal beatings of Sunday in Selma."

At left, Sheriff Clark smiles thinly and says "NEVER" to integration, while King smiles triumphantly after being granted permission by a federal judge to lead the Selma to Montgomery March. On March 21, the historic march finally begins as King leads three thousand peacefully and without incident across the Edmund Pettus Bridge and begins the fifty-four-mile trek to the state capital. The march was protected by federalized Alabama Guardsmen and U.S. Army troops. As had been agreed, after eight miles, only three hundred were allowed to continue the march. Their ranks could—and did—swell again when they came within eight miles of Montgomery.

From top left, King celebrates the bridge-crossing by stopping to pose for a picture, changes his socks during the march, and fights the rain as the march approaches its finale. Here, he and his wife lead the singing on the outskirts of Montgomery.

On March 25, a victory march begins through the streets of downtown Montgomery, winding up at the speakers' platform in front of the state capitol. With arms linked, parading down Montgomery's main street, are Ralph Bunche and the Kings. En route to the capitol, marchers sang "we have overcome today."

In front of the Alabama statehouse, before a cheering crowd of twenty-five thousand supporters from all over the nation, King exclaims, "Let us march on ballot boxes until race baiters disappear from the political arena." To roars of approval, he climaxes his speech chanting, "How long will it take?…How long? Not long. Because the arm of the moral universe is long but it bends toward justice."

From the top: Rev. Joe Carter stands guard after being the first black to register to vote in his Louisiana county in 1965. A registrar in Alabama accuses King of meddling. President Lyndon Baines Johnson shakes King's hand after signing the Voting Rights Act of 1965. At right, in rural Camden, Alabama, King urges people to register and exercise their new rights.

GETTING OUT THE VOTE
Freedom's door opens

With his children Martin III and Yolanda in tow, and escorted by his aide, Hosea Williams, King leaves a country church during his tour and greets a young man with his message: Vote. Although King had no personal interest in elected office, here he looks very much like a campaigner.

GETTING OUT THE VOTE
Freedom's door opens

*The right of citizens of the United States to vote shall not be denied
or abridged by the United States or by any State on account of race,
color, or previous condition of servitude.*

The Fifteenth Amendment, passed in 1870

A man is not a first class citizen, a number one citizen, unless he is a voter.

Rev. Joseph Carter,
St. Francisville, Louisiana, 1964

For a free people, the franchise means everything. In a democratic republic, it is the proper name of empowerment. It is the essence of political equality. Throughout the South, particularly in places where blacks outnumbered whites, those who were determined to deny this constitutional right to citizens of color found no form of terrorism too terrible if it vouchsafed voting as an exclusively white privilege.

Of the five million eligible black voters in the South in the late 1950s, only 1.3 million exercised this privilege at the ballot box. From its inception, the SCLC identified voter registration as one of its two primary theaters for direct action (the other was desegregation). In 1958 it launched a Crusade for Citizenship aimed at setting up voting clinics across the South and documenting the efforts by whites to disenfranchise blacks. The goal was to register ten million blacks before the elections in 1960. King insisted that when his people had the full power of the ballot box, it would advance the cause of both blacks and whites. He said, "We have learned in the course of our freedom struggle that the needs of twenty million Negroes are not truly separable from those of the nearly two hundred million whites…all of whom will benefit from a color-blind land of plenty that provides for the nourishment of each man's body, mind and spirit."

But the obstructionist efforts by the segregationists, long entrenched in some counties and formidable, were based on fear tactics (what King listed as "the gun, the club, and the cattle prod") dating back to the days of Reconstruction. Blacks who attempted to register were beaten. Or hanged. They had snakes dropped on them as they stood in line to register. They faced preposterous "literacy tests" (when many illiterate whites were registered). State poll taxes (these were not outlawed in federal elections until passage of the Twenty-fourth Amendment in 1964). And economic reprisals. Their homes were burned, their families driven out of town.

Armed with the new Voting Rights Act, King toured rural counties in 1966 to make sure newly enfranchised black voters registered, then voted. He was enthusiastically and respectfully greeted by the large crowds who came to see him and participate in yet another, more traditional, form of direct action. So sweeping were the provisions of the law that for counties with proven patterns of racial discrimination federal registrars and FBI agents supervised and oversaw the electoral process. Illiterate blacks could even vote orally. That year voters elected the first black sheriff in the rural deep South in this century, Thomas Gilmore.

Standing at the Selma bridge thirty-five years after Bloody Sunday, celebrating those who had marched across it, President Clinton noted that not only had nine thousand black officials been elected in the South since then, but that if King had not freed us all, two white southerners, himself and Jimmy Carter, could never have become president.

*Voters, most of them about to cast their first-ever ballots,
line up at the courthouse in Camden, Alabama, in 1966.*

Above, right: *Under the new law, one of the first African Americans casts his vote in Camden.*

Right: *In 1976, Prince Arnold of Camden becomes the first black sheriff elected in the twentieth century in this predominantly black southern county.*

JOURNEYS
His odyssey for peace and equality

This is a calling that takes me beyond national allegiances.

Martin Luther King, Jr., 1967

Few men in the twentieth century seem as washed by all waters as Martin Luther King, Jr., whose travels during the thirteen years of his public life took him from Montgomery to Memphis, from cramped jail cells in the Jim Crow South to English cathedrals, from America's inner-city ghettos to ashrams in India. And the range of humanity touched by his life and vision—politicians, the rural poor, celebrities, and heads of state—appears, in retrospect, to include all of mankind's colors, classes, and castes.

We can only wonder: How did he do it? What inner resources enabled him—as a private citizen—to travel tens of thousands of miles each month, back and forth in a country as divided as it had been during the Civil War, maintaining a schedule more suited for a president than a preacher, and then to tirelessly traverse the entire war-wracked planet, West and East, delivering to thousands his unique message of redemption, brotherly love, and social revolution?

Perhaps these photos of his globe-trotting provide a clue. Here, remarkably, was a genuinely universal man in black skin.

King dozes as he and Andrew Young, his closest aide, wait for a plane. King ceaselessly crisscrossed the nation and the world raising funds and speaking out for equality and peace.

Ghana, 1957

The Kings attend the country's independence celebration at the invitation of new president Kwame Nkrumah.

India, 1959

They meet Prime Minister Jawaharlal Nehru and, at right, King doffs his shoes before entering a shrine for Mohandas Gandhi.

Birmingham, 1960
Kenneth Kaunda, future president of Zambia, visits King and meets with members of the press.

New York City, 1962
Sharing a laugh with Bob Hope.

St. Augustine, 1964
In a Florida jail with regular cellmate Abernathy.

Detroit, 1963
At Cobo Hall rallying support for the March on Washington.

Jackson, 1963
In the funeral procession in Mississippi for Medgar Evers.

London, 1964
Preaching at St. Paul's Cathedral.

The Vatican, 1964
King and Abernathy at a private audience with Pope Paul IV.

Atlantic City, 1964
Outside the Democratic National Convention.

Washington, D.C., 1964
With Malcolm X, the only time they met.

Berlin, 1964
Bearing witness to a divided city and country.

Watts, 1965
Trying to restore calm after the riots in California.

New York City, 1965
Enjoying Sammy Davis, Jr's company.

United Nations, 1966
Speaking out, characteristially.

Chicago, 1966
With Elijah Muhammad, leader of the Nation of Islam.

Mississippi, 1966
Marching to protest the shooting of James Meredith.

Coming full circle to serve a short sentence for a conviction dating to the Birmingham protests. He is armed with his Bible.

I've been in many demonstrations all across the South,
but I can say that I have never seen,
even in Mississippi and Alabama,
mobs as hostile and as hate-filled as I've seen in Chicago.

Martin Luther King, Jr.,
Chicago, 1966

Here the enemy was not only the redneck,
sometimes it was the black face. It was
all those forces that represented the self-interest
in perpetuating the evil machine.

Jesse Jackson

How strange that Chicago, the country's "Second City," could be Albany all over again, especially after the stunning conquest in Selma.

One might think, looking at King's inaugural campaign in the North, that the lessons of his victories in three Alabama cities had been forgotten. Or perhaps it was simply the fact that those southern lessons—and Gandhian satyagraha (soul force)—couldn't be easily grafted onto big-shouldered, hog-butchering, industrialized Bigger Thomas country. As I described in my fourth novel, *Dreamer*, in 1966 Chicago was an ethnically balkanized city with a murder rate of slightly more than two people per day (so I learned when working as a *Chicago Tribune* intern in the late 1960s). It was the home of Elijah Muhammad's Nation of Islam and young militant blacks (some in gangs like the Cobras, Vice Lords, and Black Stone Rangers) for whom nonviolence in the face of white racism was perceived as unacceptable, if not downright unmanly—youths inspired by Stokely Carmichael's chant of "black power" the month before during the Mississippi march. It was a city where Negroes earned an average of $4,700 yearly and some black families were crammed ten to a flat—for the privilege of such claustrophobic lodgings slumlords charged them $90 per month. Blacks were squeezed into 10 percent of the city, with only 4 percent living in the suburbs, where homes ran as high as $15,000. No, this was worlds away from Alabama. Among its most notable former residents was Al Capone. Politically, it was the fiefdom of Mayor Richard "Boss" Daley, who cheered King's successes in the South but was not about to acknowledge severe racial problems in his own bailiwick, oh no; and it was the home for blacks more intimately familiar with (and beholden to) the Daley Machine and ward politics than King.

Who, as in Albany, arrived in Chicago in January 1966 without crisply defined goals or an original script sensitive to this city's unique spirit and complex history. Here the villains were not rural buffoons like Connor and Clark. They were abstract, faceless institutions: banks, real-estate agents, insurance companies, and white landlords barely better off than their black tenants. To demonstrate the plight of the city's poor, the SCLC (headed in Chicago by Jesse Jackson) and the Coordinating Council of Community Organizations (CCCO) leased for King and his family a Lawndale flat at 1550 South Hamlin Street, a place so unpleasant his wife sighed, "There's nothing green in sight." As the campaign drew on, King saw in his children the gradual toll that can be taken by slums and concrete and de facto segregation.

For good reason the Chicago campaign is only briefly sketched in many movement histories. On July 1 King addressed an audience of thirty-five thousand at Soldier Field, then led them to City Hall where, like his namesake Martin Luther four centuries earlier, he fastened his demands for the poor on the door—a list that included public school integration, increasing the budget for schools, expanding mass transit, building cheap public housing, and support for black banks. But a few days later, when police turned off the fire hydrants black kids played in to escape the withering Midwestern heat, the city erupted in a riot, leaving two dead and hundreds in detention. The National Guard was called in, and King spent three hellish nights rushing from one burning slum to another, pleading with young rioters to stop.

Undaunted, he continued the marches through white neighborhoods, populated by Polish, German, and Italian residents who constantly fought among themselves but bonded long

Inspired by the way Gandhi lived as a simple villager in rural India, King moved his wife and children into a slum apartment. The Kings found the Lawndale slum very oppressive. He describes his life: "I found myself fighting a daily battle against the depression and hopelessness which the heart of our cities pumps into the bloodstream of our daily lives."

King shoots pool with Chicago teenagers, trying to gain their trust and support for his nonviolent campaign against segregation in the North. He was trounced badly in a game at this time, and he realized that disuse had eroded his old pool-shark skills.

"LEARN, BABY, LEARN"
INSURE YOUR FUTURE
RETURN TO SCHOOL IN '66

BACK·TO·SCHOOL·STAY·IN·SCHOOL
★ **WEEK CAMPAIGN** ★

Sponsored by **YOUR CHICAGO URBAN LEAGUE**

4500 S. MICHIGAN AVE., CHICAGO, ILL., AT 5-5800

Left: *At a press conference, King criticizes Chicago's substandard black schools. In the photos above, he and his wife call attention to the abysmal living conditions of Chicago's poor as they help activists clean up a building in a west side ghetto. At right, top, he confronts a building superintendent.*

Right: *It was activist Al Raby, seen here, who invited King to the city. On the next spread, we see one of King's early speeches after arriving. He spoke in twenty neighborhoods in his first forty-eight hours in Chicago; he told reporters he had spoken more in a few days than he had in his entire life.*

enough (urged to do so by George Lincoln Rockwell, head of the American Nazi Party) to pour from their homes, hysterically screaming venomous racial obscenities at the marchers. Gun sales soared in Slavic neighborhoods. During one such trek of six hundred people from Marquette Park, with gang members recruited as nonviolent marshals, King was struck in the head by a rock and was barely missed by a knife thrown in his direction.

Cicero was long known as a no-man's land for the black. Indeed, when I was growing up in Evanston, Illinois, it was commonly understood that it was prudent for a black person to gas up before entering Cicero, then pray the car did not break down before the town's last street was in the rearview mirror. King and the other leaders declared they would march there. Cook County Sheriff Richard Ogilvie rightly called this idea "suicide." King refused to back down. That meant Mayor Daley had to come to the conference table to avoid a bloodbath. The meeting took place at the Palmer House. Among its participants were members of the Chicago Real Estate Board, the Housing Authority, SCLC, Archbishop John Cody, and business leaders. In the Summit Agreement they hammered out promises for the city to promote fair housing practices, encourage legislation, and make color-blind bank loans.

For some members of SNCC and CORE the agreement was a sellout. It had no guarantees, no schedule, nothing but good intentions. Without King's endorsement, CORE sent two hundred protesters into lily-white Cicero in September, protected by National Guardsmen. The violence was severe, and the marchers were forced to fall back to Lawndale.

"Morally," King said at a west side church after the Summit Agreement, "we ought to have what we say in the slogan 'freedom now.' But it doesn't all come now. That's a sad fact of life you will have to live with." Seeds that would require years to grow were at least planted during the Chicago campaign, activism that blossomed into a local chapter of Operation Breadbasket, directed by Jesse Jackson, then Operation PUSH (People United to Save Humanity).

Chicago signaled yet another, perhaps more troubling (for King) change in the racial temperature of the times. The zeitgeist of black activism was clearly moving away from nonviolent civil disobedience and brotherhood. (King was booed by some blacks in Chicago.) Perhaps King, even he, sensed that the hour for his idealistic, morally demanding philosophy of reconciliation and redemption and personal transcendence was over, and that the new, reactionary winds of social change would never blow Gandhian or Galilean notes again in his lifetime.

On July 21, thirty-five thousand gather at Chicago's Soldier Field to hear King speak. Militantly he says, "Freedom is never voluntarily granted by the oppressor: it must be demanded by the oppressed." He reaffirms his commitment to nonviolence, which he thinks "is a major factor in the creation of a moral climate that has made progress possible."

King addresses a rally in a Chicago sub-
urb. At one rally he was booed by young
blacks, something that had never before
occurred. After brooding about it, he
ruefully realized that the movement had
promised a bright future for many years,
but in the slums of Chicago it was clear it
had not delivered.

King begins leading a march from Marquette Park to a rally at a real-estate office in that all-white enclave. Seconds later he is struck on the right temple by a rock, falls to his knees, and is immediately surrounded by aides who attempt to shield him from a second barrage of rocks, bottles, and firecrackers. King quickly gathers his wits, and the march resumes.

King addresses the largest peace demonstration in history at the United Nations Plaza in New York City on April 15, 1967. Although he had been critical of the Vietnam War for more than a year, this was his most public break with the policies of the Johnson administration. The Spring Mobilization to End the War in Vietnam started in Central Park and concluded in front of the United Nations Building. The theme of King's speech was caught in his final words: "Stop the bombing. Stop the bombing."

PEACE MOVEMENT
Anguished by the horror of the Vietnam War

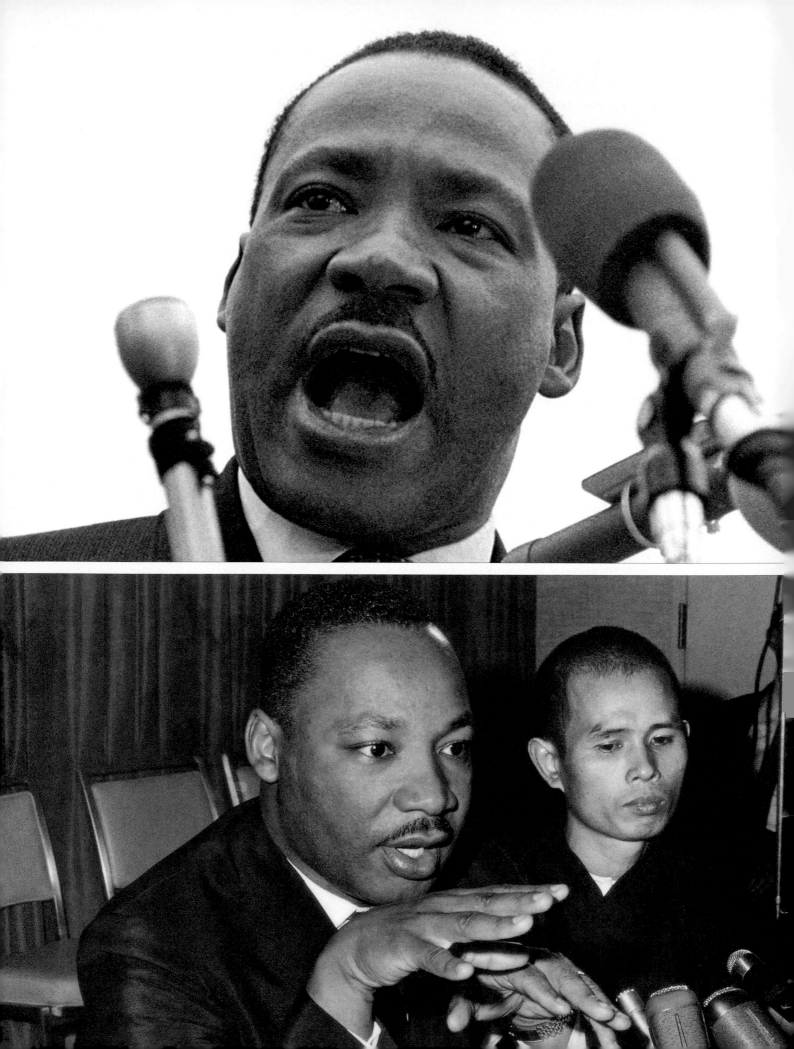

PEACE MOVEMENT
Anguished by the horror of the Vietnam War

If America's soul becomes totally poisoned, part of the autopsy must read "Vietnam."

Martin Luther King, Jr., 1967

On April 4, 1967—exactly one year to the day before his death—King delivered his first speech against the Vietnam War at New York's Riverside Church.

"Somehow, this madness must cease," he said, explaining that not only was the war diverting America's resources from ending poverty and injustice at home (to say nothing of perpetuating injustice in Vietnam), it was sending young black men "eight thousand miles away to guarantee liberties in Southeast Asia which they had not found in southwest Georgia and East Harlem." As a Christian minister, and as a recipient of the Nobel Peace Prize, King felt compelled to break his silence against America's adventurism in Vietnam and to counsel young men that "if you feel in your heart that this war is wrong…don't go and fight in it. Follow the path of Jesus Christ."

He was the first internationally celebrated American to join the antiwar movement. The backlash against his position, from whites and blacks, brought King to tears when nearly every major American newspaper and magazine condemned him for advocating a fusion of the civil rights and peace movements.

Yet others—students and young people in particular—saw the wisdom in King's prescient, principled stance. Some prayed that he and Dr. Benjamin Spock would run on a third-party presidential ticket. This King declined to do, though he continued to use every pulpit and podium to speak against the war and disregarded the hostility he received. "If you have never found something so dear and so precious to you that you will die for it," he told his congregation at Ebenezer, "then you aren't fit to live."

Opposite, top: *King calls for negotiations with the North Vietnamese during the massive UN rally: "Everyone has a duty to be in both the civil rights and the peace movements." In the bottom photograph, he holds a joint press conference with the Vietnamese Buddhist monk Thich Nhat Hahn during which he calls for a halt to American bombing in Vietnam. Below, he and other protest leaders meet with UN Undersecretary Ralph Bunche (right). On the following spread: On March 25, 1967, King and famed pediatrician Dr. Benjamin Spock, the tall, balding man with eyeglasses, lead an antiwar march in Chicago.*

ve kill men, with whom shall we
thù ta đâu có phải là người
et người đi thì ta ở với ai ?
WHILE
THE

MEMPHIS

Martyred as he crusades for the least of us

Like anybody I would like to live a long life...

Martin Luther King, Jr.,
Memphis, April 3, 1968

Martin Luther King, Jr., speaks on behalf of the sanitation workers and their demand for just treatment. At the Mason Temple in Memphis on Wednesday, April 3, he makes his chillingly prophetic "I Have Been to the Mountaintop" speech.

The penultimate chapter of King's life, set in Memphis, will always be tinctured with mystery, ringed by ambiguity and rumor. However, what we do know is this:

In February 1968, King was immersed in organizing his Poor People's Campaign, scheduled for late April when he planned to bring three thousand of America's impoverished from all backgrounds and races to the nation's capital. This would have begun, one realizes in retrospect, the third phase of his evolution—from a civil rights activist in the fifties to an antiwar proponent of peace after his Nobel Prize, and finally to his championing a Bill of Rights for the Disadvantaged and A. Philip Randolph's Freedom Budget, a domestic Marshall Plan that

might correct the evils of capitalism, which as early as 1951 King believed had outlived its usefulness. But in Memphis, thirteen hundred black sanitation workers had formed a union. The city refused to recognize it and also rejected their demands for a 10-percent wage increase and benefits. On February 12, the workers went on strike. Their grievances were real, involving racial discrimination. They were skirmishing with the police. The city brought forth an injunction to halt demonstrations. The Memphis protesters needed a high-profile champion, and King's old friend James Lawson asked him to support their efforts by delivering a speech.

King, as his close aides remarked, always had a problem with saying "no."

Thus, on March 18, he spoke to an enthusiastic crowd of seventeen thousand at the Mason Temple. He felt their enthusiasm. He believed in their cause, which combined the objectives of both the unions and black people. And didn't the plight of these sanitation workers—the lowest of the low among workers—complement the point he planned to make with the Poor People's Campaign? That night he promised if they marched, if they supported the garbagemen and their families, he would lead them.

In what should have been a triumphant overture or trial run for his April offensive in Washington, D.C.,King joined six thousand Tennesseans, who started out from the Clayborn Temple. He noticed a group of young people toward the end, holding up "Black Power Is Here" signs. That made him edgy. Many of these militant youths called themselves the Invaders and were inspired by H. "Rap" Brown's call for violent revolution. On they marched for three blocks. Then he heard young blacks in the rear looting. Breaking windows. The march deteriorated into chaos, with the Invaders battling jackbooted police in downtown Memphis. Two hundred eighty were arrested, sixty-two wounded, and one 16-year-old boy killed. As a distraught and tired King assessed the dimensions of this new disaster from the Rivermont Hotel, he knew beyond all doubt he had to return to Memphis and lead a successful, nonviolent march. To clean this up. To make things right. If he did not, his critics would have a field day, declaring that if King could not contain violence during a demonstration in Memphis, how in heaven's name could he expect to do so in the nation's capital?

He set the date: April 8. As with all his campaigns before, Memphis city officials secured an injunction barring the demonstration. And as usual King ignored it.

He returned to Memphis on April 3, checking into room 306 at the black-owned Lorraine Motel. That night he was scheduled to speak at the Mason Temple, but he was exhausted and instead sent Abernathy to address the crowd of two thousand. As it turned out, they wanted King. No one else. So he struggled out of his pajamas, dressed, and was driven to the temple in pounding rain with Andrew Young and Jesse Jackson. In that place, on that night, he delivered his last and most haunting speech:

"I've seen the promised land," he said. "And I may not get there with you. But I want you to know tonight that we, as a people, will get to the promised land." He concluded, "And I'm happy tonight. I'm not worried about anything.…Mine eyes have seen the glory of the coming of the Lord."

When he was finished, he seemed to fall, emptied, toward Abernathy, who rushed with outstretched arms to embrace and steady him.

King spent the next day (Thursday) conferring in a second-floor room at the Lorraine Motel with those whom we today might call his trusted, nonviolent "samurai." In late afternoon, he began preparing to travel with his aides to Rev. Samuel Kyle's house for dinner.He stepped outside to the balcony, and spoke to members of their group gathered down below in the parking lot. At that moment a metal-jacketed 30.-06 bullet brought down the most influential American citizen in the second half of the twentieth century: the black man who became the complex symbol for the far-reaching movement that realized the Founders' unfulfilled promises in that first revolution in 1776, completed the unfinished business of the Civil War, inspired freedom fighters in South Africa and Czechoslovakia in 1989, and provided in its methods and strategies the impetus for women's rights in the seventies and gay rights in the eighties and nineties.

At St. Joseph's Hospital he was pronounced dead at 7:05 P.M. He was only thirty-nine years old.

In 1968, striking Memphis sanitation workers walk a picket line before National Guardsmen bearing fixed bayonets. To the strikers the signs stating "I AM A MAN" were their way of saying, if you recognize my union, you recognize me.

On Wednesday, Hosea Williams, Jesse Jackson, Martin Luther King, Jr., and Ralph Abernathy gather on the balcony of the Lorraine Motel while taking a break during their planning for a march in support of the sanitation men.

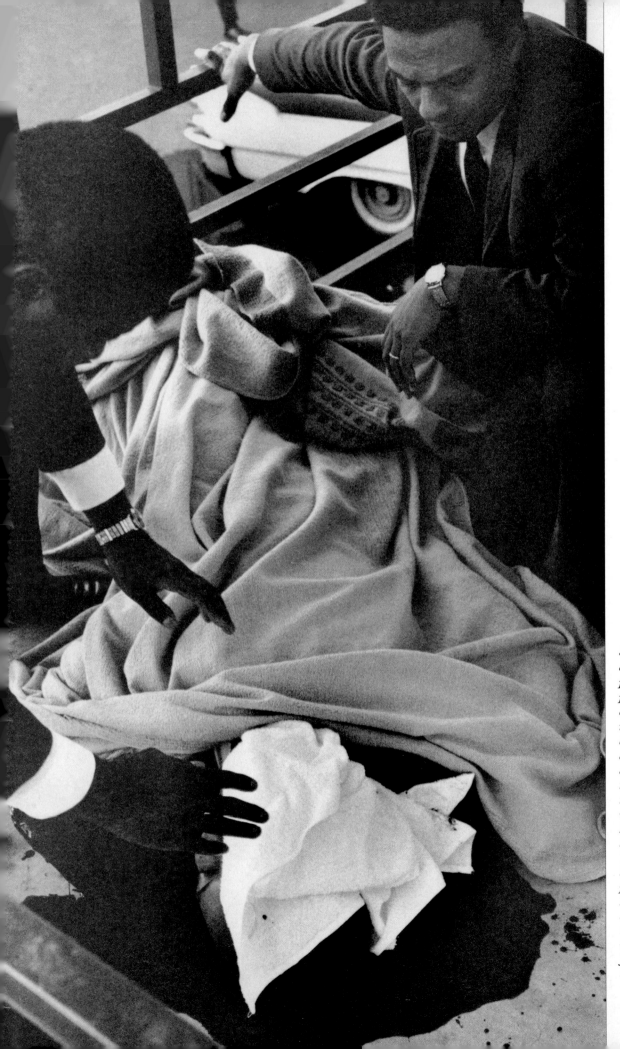

Shocked and bewildered as their leader lies in a pool of blood, King's aides point in the direction of the assasin's bullet (top), then mill hopelessly around the body as they wait for an ambulance. In the picture at left, Abernathy tires to talk to King, prostrate on the ground with a gaping wound in his jaw. He thinks he sees King's lips moving but he isn't sure if he is alive. Young feels for a pulse and believes there is one. They put a towel under King's head, partially covering it, and a bedspread over him to keep him warm. King was pronounced dead at St. Joseph's Hospital less than an hour after being shot.

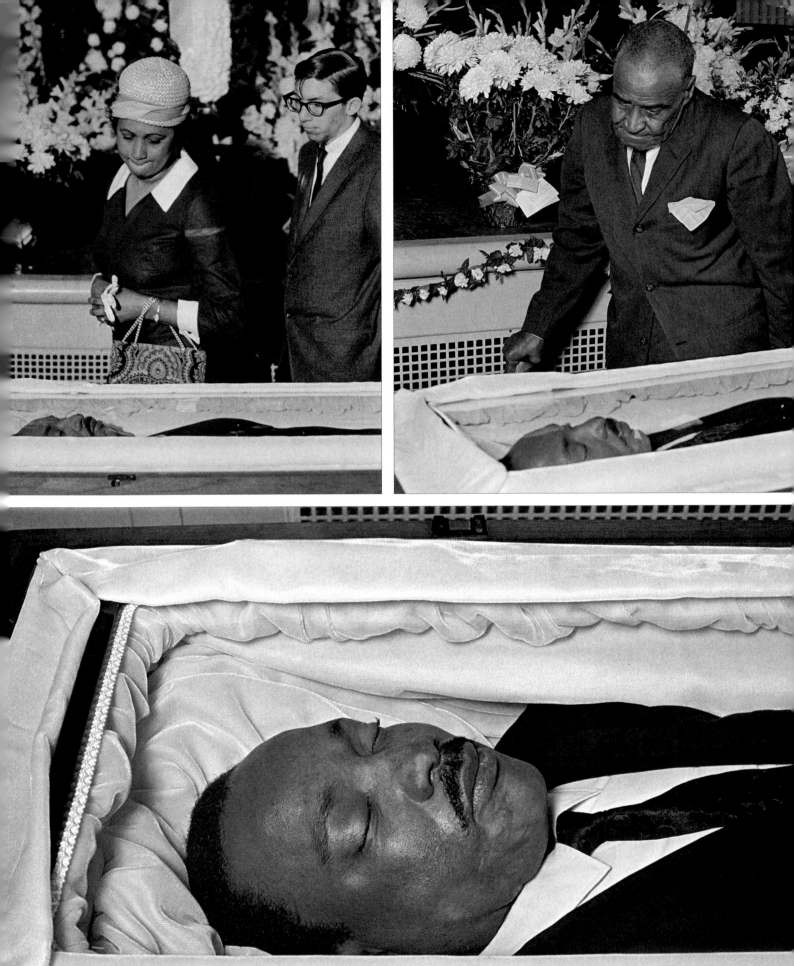

Mourners from all walks of life pay their respects and say farewell, each in their own way, to their great champion.

Martin Luther King's body is carried to the public ceremony on a simple wooden wagon drawn by mules. King's identification with the poor and disadvantaged dictated the choice of the wagon and mules and the denim clothes worn by his aides. The immense throng following the coffin honored Dr. King's memory by marching pacifically and with great dignity.

At the public service at Morehouse College, King's casket is ringed by saddened fellow activists. On the platform are ministers, friends, officials, gospel singers, and aides. Surrounding the ceremony a huge outpouring of mourners spills into the street and perches in trees and on fences to catch a glimpse of King's last rites.

ATLANTA

Home to his grave to be free

*And I guess one of the great agonies of life is that we are
constantly trying to finish that which is unfinishable.*

Martin Luther King, Jr.,
"Unfulfilled Dreams," 1968

Ironically—and tragically—on the day America's greatest advocate for peace was murdered, rioting and looting occurred in more than one hundred cities. That violence lasted for ten days. Before it ended forty-six people died, twenty-six hundred were injured, and another twenty-one hundred were arrested. The parallel with Gandhi's death was plain, and in one prescient speech, "Unfulfilled Dreams," King had mused soberly on the realization that "Gandhi had to face the fact that he was assassinated and died with a broken heart, because the nation that he wanted to unite ended up divided…"

So was America in 1968. So it is today.

Sixty thousand people gathered around Ebenezer Baptist Church for King's funeral five days after James Earl Ray's 760 Remington Gamemaster cut him down. Inside, celebrities, dignitaries, and politicians crowded the pews. A choir sang King's favorite hymns, "When I Survey the Wondrous Cross" and "In Christ There Is No East Nor West." Perhaps the high point of that day came when Abernathy played a recording of King's beautiful sermon, "The Drum Major Instinct," the essence of which is contained in the words, "There is, deep down within all of us, an instinct. It's a kind of drum major instinct—a desire to be first.…We all want to be important, to surpass others, to achieve distinction, to lead the parade.…Don't give it up." He continued, "Keep feeling the need for being first. But I want you to be first in love. I want you to be first in moral excellence. I want you to be first in generosity. That's what I want you to do.…"

Pallbearers loaded King's bier onto a flatbed wagon pulled by two mules, a symbol of the Poor People's campaign that had consumed his final days. Next: the wagon followed by fifty thousand mourners made the slow, long trek across Atlanta to Morehouse College, where one of King's earliest teachers, Rev. Benjamin Mays, delivered his eulogy.

Since the death of this great man whole libraries have been devoted to examining his life and enduring legacy. But no one spoke more beautifully about the essence of Martin Luther King, Jr.'s, life than King himself when, in "Unfulfilled Dreams," he said, "Get somebody to be able to say about you, 'He may not have reached the highest heights, he may not have realized all his dreams, but he tried.' Isn't that a wonderful thing for somebody to say about you?"

We can say all that about Martin Luther King, Jr. And we can add that the vindication of his social and philosophical vision, as a Socratic gadfly of the state, is evident in the fact that thirty-two years after his death an agency of the federal government he so consistently challenged has approved a site for his memorial on the hallowed ground of the National Mall alongside monuments to America's most revered presidents; that he is a candidate put forward to the Vatican as a martyr for the Christian faith; that a national holiday bears his name; that King County in Seattle, Washington, has been renamed after him (and no longer for Vice President William Rufus DeVane King); and that streets, buildings, and community centers from coast to coast across this vast continent, which he traversed, calling his fellow citizens to a higher ethical standard, honor his name and image.

If he did not reach the political and social Promised Land he inspired us to believe in, Martin Luther King, Jr., most certainly showed us the way.

"*I want you to say that I tried to love and serve humanity.…say that I was a drum major for justice; say that I was a drum major for peace; I was a drum major for righteousness.… I just want to leave a committed life behind.*"

ACKNOWLEDGMENTS

First, I wish to thank photographer Bob Adelman for giving me the great privilege of writing the text for these outstanding images of America's greatest civil rights leader. Of special importance among the texts from which I drew in narrating this history are Stephen B. Oates's *Let the Trumpet Sound;* volumes 1, 2, 3 of *The Papers of Martin Luther King, Jr.,* edited by Clayborne Carson; Coretta Scott King's *My Life with Martin Luther King, Jr.*; Clayborne Carson's *The Autobiography of Martin Luther King, Jr.*; James M. Washington's *The Essential Writings and Speeches of Martin Luther King, Jr.,* and *I Have a Dream: Writings and Speeches That Changed the World*; Flip Schulke's *Martin Luther King, Jr.: A Documentary—Montgomery to Memphis* (text by Penelope McPhee); King's own *Strength to Love*; Clayborne Carson's *A Knock at Midnight,* Theodore Pappas's *Plagiarism and the Culture War: The Writings of Martin Luther King, Jr., and Other Prominent Americans*; Aldon D. Morris's *The Origins of the Civil Rights Movement*; John A. Garraty's *The American Nation, A History of the United States*; and Bob Adelman's article from *Ebony,* "Birth of a Voter."

Charles Johnson
Seattle

Photographs were crucial in advancing and recording Dr. King's lifelong struggle for equality and justice for all Americans. Forty years have passed since his assassination. *Remembering Martin Luther King, Jr.,* attempts a comprehensive and intricate photographic portrait, a close look at the hero who led the great movement that helped bridge the gap between American ideals and practices.

As an activist photographer during the days of the Civil Rights Movement, I found that Dr. King unforgettably voiced my aspirations. He showed us how grievous wrongs could begin to be righted by imaginatively and righteously employing our rich tradition of peaceful protest. Only the most profound moral and religious dedication could have given Dr. King the fortitude to endure the terror and attacks that were his almost daily lot. Going through the book, keep in mind that many Civil Rights photographers shared Dr. King's idealism and did their work aware that a camera wasn't much protection. A number were jailed or hurt. One died.

Dr. King's story needed to be told as well as seen, and we are blessed to have the American master, Charles Johnson, whose radiant intelligence, vigorous prose, and passionate empathy for Dr. King's quest and vision illuminate these pages. Rick DeMonico took a bewildering variety of images and elegantly wove them into a coherent whole. His belief that there was always a good solution is demonstrated on every spread. With boundless energy and inventiveness, he produced ingenious and stylish designs. Christopher Sweet smoothed the rough places in the writing and made many savvy saves.

To draw a detailed portrait of Dr. King required searching through more than three hundred thousand photographs, a monumental task that led to fascinating glimpses of what the Civil Rights leader had to do to realize his mission. That research produced a larger earlier work edited and distilled with great inspiration and style by Will Hopkins and Mary K. Baumann, ably assisted by Mary Beth Brewer. Christopher Sweet was its brilliant impresario.

Our photographic research took us to all corners of the country. Individual photographers were extremely generous in opening their files. I'd like to express my gratitude to my pal, John Loengard, and friends Flip Schulke, Charles Moore, Bob Fitch, Ben Fernandez, Matt Herron, James Karales and Jay Leviton. Three great photographers, Dan Weiner, Paul Schutzer and James Karales, are fortunate in having widows, Sandra Weiner, Bernice Schutzer and Monica Karales, so devoted to their historic work.

Photo agencies also shared detailed knowledge of their archives. I must especially thank Paula Vogel at AP/Wide World Photos. She was generous with her rich archive and passed on much useful information. Norman Currie at Corbis was unfailingly helpful. Gary Truman, a true pro, made working at the Flip Schulke Archive completely collegial. At my agency, Magnum Photos, I'd like to particularly thank Michael Shulman for sharing his extensive knowledge and for his constant cooperation. Ben Chapnick and Richard Serviss at Black Star were resourceful and offered great assistance dealing with our numerous requests. John Broderick at the Dan Weiner Archive has been unfailingly helpful. Kathi Doak at the Time-LIFE picture collection graciously allowed us to conduct extensive, original picture research for which we are greatly in her debt. The cooperation of Eric Young at Archive Photos and Hermene Hartmann, who represents the John Tweedle Photography Collection, was invaluable.

My assistant, the photographer Stephen Watt, intelligently organized and digitized my archive. His wizardry with Photoshop, our daylight darkroom, revived many of the photographs in the book. John Horan's prudent advice helped us with some thorny issues, and Kenneth Norwick's recommendations were practical and wise.

When I showed an early version of *Remembering Martin Luther King, Jr.*, to our publisher, Richard Fraiman, he immediately saw it as a LIFE bookazine. We are grateful for his wise judgment, continuing support and for sharing the Dream. Bob Sullivan, an editor's editor, not only spotted all the problems but he had the best solutions. Judiciously, he took something away on one page and added something else to another; before we knew it, we had a LIFE book. Joy Butts and Shelley Rescober at TIHE ingeniously resolved many of the perplexities of the publishing process.

Personal heroes of mine from those terrifying and exhilarating movement days who contributed to the book are Dave Dennis, Marvin Rich, Mary Hamilton, Andy Young, and my best man and great friend, Rudy Lombard.

Bob Adelman
Miami Beach

ABOUT THE AUTHORS

A widely published literary critic, screenwriter, philosopher, cartoonist, essayist and lecturer, **Dr. Charles Johnson** is also author of several novels, including *Middle Passage* (which garnered him the 1990 National Book Award), as well as three short-story collections, the most recent being *Dr. King's Refrigerator and Other Bedtime Stories*. His many nonfiction works include *Africans in America: America's Journey Through Slavery* (coauthored with Patricia Smith), *Being and Race: Black Writing Since 1970*, *Black Men Speaking* (coedited with John McCluskey, Jr.), two books of drawings, and, most recently, *Turning the Wheel: Essays on Buddhism and Writing*. In 2007, he contributed the essays featured in *Mine Eyes Have Seen*, tracing the Civil Rights Movement. Among his many honors are a MacArthur Fellowship and an Academy Award in Literature from the American Academy of Arts and Letters. One of twelve African-American authors honored in an international series of stamps celebrating great writers of the twentieth century, he is currently the S. Wilson and Grace M. Pollock Professor of Writing at the University of Washington in Seattle.

A photographer and social activist known for his historic coverage of the Civil Rights Movement, **Bob Adelman** has also worked in efforts to alleviate poverty, reform education, expand civil liberties and document the arts. The internationally recognized photojournalist has covered social and political issues for *LIFE*, *The New York Times Magazine*, London's *Sunday Times Magazine*, *Newsweek*, *Time*, *Esquire*, *Vanity Fair*, *Paris Match* and numerous other publications. He is a Guggenheim Fellow and a National Endowment for the Arts grantee. His photographs are in the collections of major museums. He has published a number of photographic books, including *Down Home*, detailing the impact of social change on a Faulknerian town; *Street Smart*, documenting children's inventive play; *The Next America* (with Michael Harrington), offering social idealist's view of the United States; *Visions of Liberty* (with Ira Glasser), celebrating the Bill of Rights; and *King: The Photobiography of Martin Luther King, Jr.* (with Charles Johnson), telling King's life story in photographs. Most recently he assembled his gripping, provocative and moving photos into *Mine Eyes Have Seen*, a photographic journey through the Civil Rights Movement and the culture that made it possible.

PHOTOGRAPHY CREDITS

Cover	Bob Adelman
Title Page	Bob Adelman
Page 5	Bob Adelman
Page 7	Benedict J. Fernandez
Page 8	Dan Weiner
Page 9	
Top	Dan Weiner
Bottom	AP Wide World Photos
Page 10-11, 12, 13	Dan Weiner
Page 14	Bettmann/Corbis
Page 15	Paul Robertson/LIFE
Page 16-17 All (3)	Dan Weiner
Page 18	Bettmann/Corbis
Page 18-19	AP Wide World Photos
Page 20	Don Cravens/LIFE
Page 21	Bettmann/Corbis
Page 22-23 All (2)	Charles Moore/Black Star
Page 24-25	Paul Schutzer/LIFE
Page 26	
Top Left	Paul Schutzer/LIFE
Bottom Left	Bob Henriques/Magnum Photos
Center	Paul Schutzer/LIFE
Page 27, 28-29, 30-31	Paul Schutzer/LIFE
Page 32	New York Daily News
Page 33, 34-35, 36-37 All (6)	Bettmann/Corbis
Page 38-39 All (3)	James Karales
Page 40	
Top	James Karales
Bottom	Flip Schulke
Page 41	Don Uhrbrock/LIFE
Page 42-43 All (2)	Flip Schulke
Page 44-45	Jay Levitton
Page 46	
Top	Flip Schulke
Bottom	Bob Fitch
Page 47	Henri Cartier-Bresson/Magnum Photos
Page 48	
Top	Bettmann/Corbis
Bottom	AP Wide World Photos
Page 49	
Top	Don Uhrbrock/LIFE
Bottom	AP Wide World Photos
Page 50	Flip Schulke
Page 51	
Top	Charles Moore/Black Star
Bottom	Flip Schulke
Page 52-53	
Top	Bettmann/Corbis
Bottom Left	Paul Schutzer/LIFE
Bottom Right	Don Uhrbrock/LIFE
Page 54-55 All (3)	Paul Schutzer/LIFE

Page 56	
Top	AP Wide World Photos
Bottom	Paul Schutzer/LIFE
Page 57	
Top	AP Wide World Photos
Bottom	Paul Schutzer/LIFE
Page 58	AP Wide World Photos
Page 59	
Top	Don Uhrbrock/LIFE
Bottom	Bettmann/Corbis
Page 60	
Top	Don Uhrbrock/LIFE
Bottom	Bettmann/Corbis
Page 61, 62-63	AP Wide World Photos
Page 64-65	
Top (3)	Bob Adelman
Bottom	James Karales
Page 66 All (2)	James Karales
Page 67, 68, 69	AP Wide World Photos
Page 70	Bettmann/Corbis
Page 71	
Top All (3)	James Karales
Page 72 All (2)	Bob Adelman
Page 73	
Top	Charles Moore/Black Star
Bottom	Bob Adelman
Page 74	
Top Left	AP Wide World Photos
Top Right	Matt Herron/Take Stock
Bottom	Frank Dandridge/LIFE
Page 75	AP Wide World Photos
Page 76-77	Paul Schutzer/LIFE
Page 78-83 All (5)	Bob Adelman
Page 84	James Mahan/LIFE
Page 85	AP Wide World Photos
Page 86	Jay Leviton
Page 87	Bettmann/Corbis
Page 88-89, 90 All (4)	AP Wide World Photos
Page 91	Bettmann/Corbis
Page 92-93 All (4)	AP Wide World Photos
Page 95	
Top	AP Wide World Photos
Bottom Left	AP Wide World Photos
Bottom Right	Bettmann/Corbis
Page 96	Bettmann/Corbis
Page 97	AP Wide World Photos
Page 98	Charles Moore/Black Star
Page 99	Bob Adelman
Page 100, 101 All (5)	Flip Schulke
Page 102	AP Wide World Photos
Page 103-109 All (13)	Bob Adelman

Page 110	
Left Top	Bob Adelman
Left Center/Bottom	Bettmann/Corbis
Page 110-111	Bob Adelman
Page 112-113	Bob Fitch
Page 114-115 All (3)	Bob Adelman
Page 116	Bob Fitch
Page 117	
Top	Mark Kauffman/LIFE
Bottom Left	Bettmann/Corbis
Bottom Right	AP Wide World Photos
Page 118	
Top Left	Alfred Eisenstaedt/LIFE
Top Right	Archive Photos
Bottom	Bettmann/Corbis
Page 119	
Top Left	AP Wide World Photos
Top Right	John Loengard/LIFE
Bottom Left	Archive Photos
Bottom Right	Bettmann/Corbis
Page 120	
Top Left	Bettmann/Corbis
Top Right/Bottom	AP Wide World Photos
Page 121	
Top	Bettmann/Corbis
Bottom Left	AP Wide World Photos
Bottom Right	John Loengard/LIFE
Page 122 All (2)	AP Wide World Photos
Page 123	Flip Schulke
Page 124	Bettmann/Corbis
Page 126-127	Bob Fitch
Page 128 All (3)	AP Wide World Photos
Page 129	
Top	AP Wide World Photos
Bottom	Roger Malloch/Black Star
Page 130-131	John Tweedle
Page 132	AP Wide World Photos
Page 133	Roger Malloch/Black Star
Page 134-135 All (3)	Bettmann/Corbis
Page 136-137	Bob Adelman
Page 138	
Top	Bob Adelman
Bottom	AP Wide World Photos
Page 139	AP Wide World Photos
Page 140-141	AP Wide World Photos
Page 142 All (2)	AP Wide World
Page 143	Bettmann/Corbis
Page 144	
Top	Bettmann/Corbis
Bottom	AP Wide World Photos
Page 146-147 All (3)	Joseph Louw/LIFE
Page 148-157, 159 All (11)	Bob Adelman